GIVE ME
This
MOUNTAIN

Dr. R. Michael Baldock

ISBN 978-1-64515-197-5 (paperback)
ISBN 978-1-64515-198-2 (digital)

Copyright © 2019 by Dr. R. Michael Baldock

All rights reserved. No part of this publication may be reproduced, distributed, or transmitted in any form or by any means, including photocopying, recording, or other electronic or mechanical methods without the prior written permission of the publisher. For permission requests, solicit the publisher via the address below.

Christian Faith Publishing, Inc.
832 Park Avenue
Meadville, PA 16335
www.christianfaithpublishing.com

All scripture is from the King James Version of the Bible unless quoted differently.

Printed in the United States of America

A Special Thanks

I want to extend a special thanks to my wonderful wife Julie for putting up with me while I was preoccupied being in labor pushing to give birth to this book. Also, to my close friend, Pastor Tim Agee and the great congregation of The Sanctuary Church in Beech Grove/Indianapolis for their support in this Endeavour. I also want to say thank you to Mel and Erin Glenn without whom this baby (Give Me This Mountain) would not have been possible. To Apostle Anthony and First Lady Connie Williams from The Lion of Judah, Malden Missouri who encouraged me years ago to start writing. Last but certainly not least, to all my family and friends who have been a great support system to Julie and I over the years and are still there.

    Thank You Everyone

Dr. Mike Baldock

Contents

Introduction 7

Chapter 1   You Must Take a Stand! 11

Chapter 2   Must Have a Vision 21

Chapter 3   Don't Give into Distractions 29

Chapter 4   Don't Let Go of the Promise 39

Chapter 5   Endure Hard Times 47

Chapter 6   Don't Lose Your Strength 61

Chapter 7   Remain Courageous 67

Chapter 8   Don't Throw Away Your Confidence! 79

Chapter 9   Do Not Waver in Your Faith 87

Chapter 10   Stretch Your Faith 95

Chapter 11   Delays Do Not Mean No! 105

Chapter 12   It Is Finished 113

Conclusion 119

Introduction

In reading the story of Moses sending out twelve spies into the promised land (Canaan) when they returned, there was a man by the name of Caleb that was one of two that brought back a good report. I was so intrigued with this man Caleb that I began to follow his life in the scriptures. At the ripe age of eighty-five when Joshua was dividing the inheritances to Israel, Caleb proclaimed, "**Give me this mountain!**" It was his description of himself that prompted me to write this book.

Within the pages of this book comes the revelation of the courage it takes for a person to hold on to the promises of God. It is rare that anything in life comes easy. Most of the time, it takes hard work and perseverance to obtain our dreams and overcome the obstacles that we may face in life. I can still hear my mother saying, "When you spill your own sweat, blood, and tears to gain something, you will respect and appreciate it more than if it was just handed to you." Her words were so true.

Although we have the promises of God before us, there is often a battle to receive them. By a battle, I am talking about the enemy doing everything he can to keep the believer from walking in those promises. It has been said, "Good things come to those who wait." While this may be true, it is the waiting that most of us don't want to do. However, if we do wait, there is a reward at the end. Caleb waited forty-five years to take possession of Mount Horeb. When he first saw this great mountain, he was forty years of age; now at eighty-five, he is ready to take this mountain as his own.

We often think of someone at the age of eighty-five to have their best years behind them. Yet, Caleb's best years were ahead of him. The Bible is filled with people who waited years for the promises of God to come to pass. I have no idea how long you have been waiting on your mountain, but I want to encourage you to continue to hold fast to what God has promised.

There are times when a person has to reach within themselves and find the, courage, hope, and faith that the word of God supplies and to go for their dreams and desires. One of the many things that I discovered about Caleb was his intense desire for an inheritance that was promised, not only for the nation of Israel, but for him as an individual. The scriptures proclaimed:

"Delight thyself in the Lord and He shall give you the desires of thine heart." Psalm 37:4

The term *"Delight thyself also in the Lord"* denotes the idea of "becoming soft and pliable in the hands of God" who is the Potter as we are the clay, and conforming to His will. The following scripture brings revelation to this statement;

"Commit thy way unto the Lord; trust also in Him, and He shall bring it to pass." Psalm 37:5

What a promise that is set before us! The key word in the above passage is "*commit*." It is from the Hebrew word "*ghalal*" meaning to whirl, to roll, turn, to be rolled together, to roll oneself upon; to be rolled (in blood), to be dyed red. The picture is rolling oneself upon the Lord, trusting and committing one's life to the Lord. When I read this definition, it takes my mind to a passage of scripture in the New Testament in which, not only confirmed what the writer said in Psalm 37, but sealed it.

"I beseech you therefore, brethren, by the mercies of God." Nothing can be accomplished through any works or merit on the behalf of you and I. i.e. the believer, they are only obtained because of a **"Merciful God,"** the phrase *"that ye present your bodies"* (position yourself for a God opportunity), when the believer presents himself, he is giving the Holy Spirit latitude to work and lead in

his life, in becoming a living sacrifice, (the term *"a living sacrifice"* is dealing with being made conformable to the death and resurrection of Christ (see Romans 6:3–6), this cannot be accomplished without the leadership of the Holy Spirit within the life of the believer), holy (sanctified, which is done initially upon a person receiving Jesus Christ [being born again] and continues [ongoing] within the life of the believer), acceptable unto God (denotes the believer as presenting his body as the "temple of God" without which He will not receive), which is your reasonable service (Because of the finished work of Jesus Christ at the cross, this is not an unreasonable request, i.e. demand).

Every believer must make and live a committed life to God in order to receive and walk in the "inheritance" that has been made available through and by Jesus Christ. Our faith must have the finished work of Jesus Christ at Calvary as its object. With this all being said, let's begin to examine just how it was that Caleb was able to hold on those forty-five years.

In the following pages, we are going to discover why Caleb was able to wait and not let go of this "mountain." What was it that drove him? How was he able to hold on? These questions and more are what we are going to address. I am excited to share with you the revelation that the Holy Spirit gave me concerning Caleb and what drove him to get his mountain. You too can obtain your mountain!

Chapter 1

You Must Take a Stand!

"Let us hold fast the profession of our faith without wavering, for He is faithful that promised." Hebrews 10:23

I once heard the statement, *"If you won't stand for something, you will fall for anything!"* In my experience, I have found that to be so true. We live in a society that can be so easily swayed from one thing to another and that is scary. People seem to be tossed about like the waves of the sea. I have seen so many fads come and go and so many Christians falling prey to a slick tongue evangelist or a so-called prophet that it causes something to rise up inside of me.

In the late seventies and early eighties, there was a well-renowned minister (I use that term loosely) who was teaching his people to live strictly by faith, however, the faith he taught was misplaced faith. His teaching was that the people had no need for doctors, that God would take care of them. Sounded great but was misleading. After there were several stillborn babies being birthed in homes by a midwife, CPS got involved. They discovered a tremendous loss of life, not only for the babies but also for some mothers dying while giving birth. It caused a great uproar in the Christian community. It was not long after this occurrence that the leader himself took ill. This revealed the truth. While he had been teaching and preaching that they had no need for doctors, it came out that he had a private physician. There has to be a special place for people like that. Many were moved and swayed by his personality and deception, not to mention those that lost their lives.

Let me share another story that I was involved in firsthand. When the *"faith message"* came on the scene like a rushing wind, many were held captive by the name and claimed its message. Thousands if not millions bought into this prosperity message. I want to insert this. I believe that God wants the believer to prosper and be in health in their journey. However, that does not mean that our success as a Christian is measured by our bank account, the house we live in, and the cars and suits we may possess. I agree that this life that I now live, I must live it by faith. But that being said, it must be faith in the correct object which is the cross and what Jesus Christ accomplished there. Let me get back to my original thought concerning the so-called faith message. One of the scriptures that was often quoted was Romans 4:17.

> *"As it is written, I have made thee a father of many nations, before him whom he believed, even God, who quickeneth the dead, and calleth those things which be not as though they were." Romans 4:17*

The last phrase of this passage is what thousands were holding onto and **"calleth those things which be not as though they were."** People were going around trying to call things into existence and many were deceived and disappointed and suffered loss. Before I go any further, let me insert my thought. I do agree that when walking in faith, we must come into agreement with the word, and the word must be in our heart, mind, and soul. But, that word must be in its proper setting and context. In the above passage, I want you to notice something very important. It was not the believer (Abraham) calling those things; it was God calling those things that were not as though they were. Listen closely: if God hasn't called it, you can't call it. However, if God has called it, you can "stand on it" just as Abraham did.

I had a family in the church that I was pastoring, and they had bought into this so-called faith message hook, line, and sinker. They had a son that was born with a heart defect. He would often turn blue to a lack of oxygen. At the age of five, they took him to a great hospital to undergo surgery. They had been holding onto "calling those things which be not as though they were." With all of the positive confession and doing what the so-called faith message taught, their son died on the operating table. What a devastation they now faced. Do we get mad at God for not giving him a new heart? Do we get angry with ourselves for bringing him to this hospital? Do we get angry at the doctors for not saving him? There was a mountain of emotions that ran through them. I don't have the answer as to why their precious son died, but I do know that God is still God, and His word is true.

Another great concern of mine is the message of the modern-day church. I could write a book just about that. It sickens me how the modern-day church, the secret sensitive church, has watered down the gospel of Jesus Christ. Sin is rarely preached; some teach that once a person is born again, they no longer have a sin conscious, and others teach once saved always saved. A lot of today's messages are no more than motivational speeches. I am not against motivating people, but if we are to be motivated, it must be by the Word of God. It is "the truth" that makes the believer free. The believer must not waver in their faith.

Romans 4:18–22 describes the stand that must be taken:

1. Against hope, he (Abraham) yet believed on hope.
2. He was not weak in faith.
3. He did not consider the deadness of his body nor the deadness of Sarah's womb.
4. He did not stagger at the promises of God through unbelief.
5. He was fully persuaded that what God had promised He (God) was able to perform.
6. Because of his unwavering faith (making a stand), it was imputed to him for righteousness.

Taking a stand is one of the reasons why I am referring to Caleb. The Holy Spirit revealed to me some qualities that this great man possessed. Caleb had to make a stand that was contrary to an entire generation. He and Joshua alone were the only survivors of a generations of unbelievers. The story began in Numbers chapter thirteen.

Moses sent out twelve men to spy the layout of the land of Canaan. He instructed them to see the land and the people that dwell there, whether they were strong or weak, few or many. They were to look at the land and see if it would be a place to live in. After forty days, the twelve came back with a report of what they saw. At the beginning, the report was good. They brought back a cluster of grapes that took two men to carry. I was convinced that these two men were Joshua and Caleb, although the scripture does not name them as such. They told Moses and Aaron that the land was a land that flowed with milk and honey.

However, before anyone could get too excited, they came across with the negative word *"nevertheless."* Now came the complaining; the people were strong that dwell there; the children of Anak lived there (possibly giants), the Amalakites, the Hittites, the Jebusites, the Amorites etc. Don't you hate it when someone rains on your parade? That was exactly what ten of the spies did. Have you ever been excited about something only to have someone throw a wet blanket on your fire?

It was then that Caleb spoke up, but it did not stop those from continuing with their rampage. They continued with their negative talk to the degree that they referred to themselves as *"grasshoppers."* Before we examine Caleb's statements, let me share the following:

There are two kinds of people that you will encounter in life. They are what I call *"basement people and balcony people."* The basement people are those who use the word *"nevertheless"* and begin to show all of the reasons why you can never accomplish your dreams. Then there is the balcony people. These are the people who are there to cheer you on and help you live your dream and get your mountain. Thank God for the *"balcony people!"*

Caleb did not allow these basement people to keep him from what God had promised. Notice what Caleb said.

1. **He stilled the people.** It is important to close out the negative people in your life. Nothing good ever comes from a negative report that becomes a roadblock to what God has promised.
2. **He proclaimed,** *"Let us go up at once and possess the land!"*
3. *"We are well able to overcome it!"* I have noticed, when we hesitate in faith, it gives the enemy opportunity to show the negatives and remove us from focusing on the promise.

I call what Caleb proclaimed as *"immediate faith."* Immediate faith is a now faith. It is a faith that presses on, no matter the surroundings. I am reminded of two occasions in the scriptures where immediate faith is exercised. First, there was a man that was paralyzed and laid on a bed his entire life. When word came that Jesus was in a house he had four friends take him there. When they arrived, the crowd was so great that they could not get him in to Jesus. They took him up to the roof and made a hole and lowered him down before Jesus, and he received his deliverance and healing (Luke 5:18–20). Another example was when the Gentile woman came before Jesus concerning her daughter that was vexed with a demon spirit. Her faith was *"immediate faith,"* and her daughter received a miracle (Matthew 15:21–28).

Faith is not based on what we see but by what Jesus Christ finished at the cross. We cannot place our faith on what some preacher has said (if it doesn't line up with the Word of God) nor on the opinions of others. The apostle Paul made this abundantly clear to the Galatians:

> *"I am crucified with Christ; nevertheless, I live; yet not I, but Christ liveth in me: and the life that I now live in the flesh I live by the faith of the Son of God, who loved me, and gave Himself for me." Galatians 2:20*

* * * * *

Contend for the Faith

"Beloved, when I gave all diligence to write unto you of the common salvation, it was needful for me to write unto you, and exhort you that ye should earnestly contend for the faith which was once delivered unto the saints." Jude 3

Let's closely examine the above passage of scripture, to gain a clear understand to what the Holy Spirit conveyed to Jude. The term, *"when I gave all diligence"* reveals the urgency that the Holy Spirit placed within Jude to write this. Jude had first considered writing concerning the common salvation as noted in his following statement, *"to write unto you of the common salvation."* However, the Holy Spirit had another direction for Jude.

The next statement revealed the direction in which the Holy Spirit was compelling Jude to address. *"It was needful for me to write unto you,"* The language used here was stronger in its compulsion than the one previously given. I believe that this revealed to the redirection that the Holy Spirit gave to the writer. He was telling Jude that there was a more compelling situation to address. This was made known by the next statement, *"and exhort you,"* The word *"exhort"* is from the Greek word *"parakaleo"* which is a compound word; the first word *"para,"* which means side by side. The next word is *"kaleo,"* meaning to call. Putting these two words together, it is defined as to call to one's side, hence to aid. It is used for every kind of calling to a person which is intended to produce a particular effect, comfort, exhort, desire, called for.

In other words, the Holy Spirit came alongside Jude, compelling him to write on the subject that was needed at that time, the statement, *"ye should earnestly contend for the faith."* The phrase, *"earnestly contend,"* is derived from the Hebrew word *"epagonizomia,"* meaning the idea of vigorously, intensely approach something with the idea a determined struggle to defeat what is opposing, **"The Faith."** It is interesting to note, this is the only place in the New Testament that this word was used. Our English word "**agony**," is from this term (word).

Notice that the believer is too "*contend*" for "*the faith*." The term "*the faith*" is one of great importance, especially for the believer. This term is recorded forty times in the New Testament (KJV). Thirty-eight times, it is referring to "**the Cross and the Finished Work of Jesus Christ.**" It also refers to the Doctrine of Christianity, which is the very gospel that the apostle Paul spoke of in 1 Corinthians 1:17,18, and 23. As a believer, we are to use every effort with an intensity to defend, i.e. contend for the faith. We (the body of Christ), the church, must rise up against anything that opposes and or is watering down, sugar coating, and trying to pervert this great gospel.

* * * * *

Stand, Do Not Retreat

In making a bold stand, it takes being equipped with the right armor. The apostle Paul revealed through the Holy Spirit just how we (the believer) are to be equipped. See Ephesians 6:10–18.

"Finally, my brethren, be strong in the Lord, and in the power of His might." Ephesians 6:10

What an awesome command! *"Be strong in the Lord, and the power of His might."* This command comes with the idea of not only "*standing firm*" in all that God has promised, but to do so in what Jesus Christ accomplished at the cross, which is "*the power of His might.*" It also confirms that the believer cannot in any way walk in a life of victory, obtaining their mountain within their own strength, ability, knowledge, or wisdom. To walk in the promises of God (obtaining your mountain), the believer must relinquish (deny) himself and ever keep Jesus Christ and the cross as their object of faith.

> *"Wherefore take unto you the whole armor of God, that ye may be able to withstand in the evil day, and having done all stand." Ephesians 6:13*

Taking on (applying) the whole armor of God is of the utmost importance in standing and not retreating. Without the armor that God has supplied, the believer find themselves defeated and unable to gain their mountain. The next phrase at the beginning of verse 14, "*Stand therefore,*" was not a request nor a hopeful thought, but rather a command. It becomes the believer's choice to do the following:

1. **Having your loins gird about with truth;** this is not speaking of just truth, but rather, the truth. It is the truth of the gospel that stabilizes the believer.
2. **Having on the breastplate of righteousness;** it is the breastplate of righteousness that keeps one's heart right and guides them in a right way of living.
3. **Your feet shod with the preparation of the gospel of peace.** This represents walking and participating in the true word of God. The gospel is a continuing guide used by the Holy Spirit to direct the life of the believer.
4. **Taking the shield of faith;** this shield provides the believer with the ability to stand against anything that the enemy may come at you with. Notice, it "quenches all the fiery darts of the wicked."
5. **Take the helmet of salvation.** If there is one area that needs protection, it is the mind of the believer. I believe that the mind is one of the first place the enemy attacks. We are admonished as believers to renew our minds and to think properly (Romans 12:2; Philippians 4:8).
6. **The sword of the Spirit which is the Word of God.** It is the word of God that clears the path of the believer. Don't start your day without the word of God going before you.
7. **Praying always with all prayer and supplication in the Spirit.** A life of prayer is essential for every believer.

Prayer is simply communication with God. Believers are instructed to pray without ceasing (1 Thessalonians 5:17).

* * * * *

Challenge!

I am convinced that Caleb had faith and confidence in God to bring Israel into the land with victory. He looked beyond the walled cities and the strength of the inhabitants of the land. He was focused on the milk and honey and the great cluster of grapes. There was something else that grabbed the attention of Caleb; that was Mount Hebron. Caleb kept his mind and faith geared toward the promised inheritance that God had given. Caleb looked toward the promise. While the believer of today must look back at the **"Cross"** from which all blessings flow! The cross is the means of all that we ever need in our walk of faith while Jesus Christ is the source.

Caleb Stood His Ground!
Now, It Is Time For You To Take A Stand!

Chapter 2

Must Have a Vision

"Where there is no vision, the people perish: but he that keepeth the law happy is he." Proverbs 29:18

From the first day that Caleb saw Mount Hebron, he made up his mind that it belonged to him. He took heart in what Moses said to him, "*Wherever your feet walks, that land is your inheritance.*" The vision of Mount Hebron was part of the driving force that gave Caleb the strength to continue. It did not matter what happened during the forty years of wandering in the wilderness; he continually kept this vision before him.

Having a vision in life is extremely important, for without it, a person continues to wander without any direction. It gives the person something to hold onto.

Webster describes vision as the act or power of sensing with the eyes, the power of anticipating that which may come to be foresight, something seen in or as if in a dream, often attributed to divine agency, vivid imaginative anticipation; and something seen, an object of sight.

The Hebrew word for vision is "*chazon*," meaning a mental sight, a dream, a vision, a revelation, an oracle, a prophecy.

Having a vision is the ability to look beyond where you are now and see where you are headed. It is the eyesight of the mind that brings hope and desire, which allows the believer to see things that God desires for them (us). It is the ultimate goal for one to strive for. It often begins with a mental picture. Having a vision creates a motivation toward the things of God. The good news is; vision is not bound by our past nor is it limited to our natural limitations. It can be the visualization of your breakthrough. I perceive vision as seeing the blessings of God coming alive in our personal living. It is exciting when you can see yourself becoming what God has proclaimed that you are. Just as Caleb visualized himself obtaining and living on Mount Hebron, so can you hold onto the mountain God has given you through the "**Finished Work of Jesus Christ at Calvary!**"

Having a vision is not limited to a mental picture; it is becoming actively involved in that vision which we will discuss later in this chapter. It is seeing yourself with the God-given ability to accomplish what you see. Caleb saw himself everyday as taking possession and occupying his mountain. Sometimes it is easy to see what God has for you yet not that easy to do. This is especially true if one does not enjoy waiting on the vision.

It is important to not allow anything to cloud your vision. There are a number of things in this life that will try to cloud and remove us from the vision. Have you noticed how difficult it is to drive a vehicle in the midst of heavy-cloud coverage? It makes traveling extremely dangerous. It can be easy to lose your way in a fog. This is not only true in the natural but even more so in the spiritual. There are a number of things that can become a cloud which we will deal with in the proceeding chapters.

I can just imagine how difficult it must have been for Caleb to continue holding his vision of Mount Hebron. He was forty years old when he first saw the mountain, and he was eighty-five when it became a reality. He lived through forty years of wandering in the wilderness, waiting on a generation of unbelievers to die off. During those forty years, I am sure there was a lot of negative talk. After all, he was living around a bunch of people filled with doubt and unbelief. Living around a bunch of complainers had to be difficult at times, yet he held on to his vision. I know for myself, I can't stand being around people who complain all of the time. If you allow them, they strip you of any positives in life including your vision.

*****

Making Your Vision a Reality

1. Stretching your faith.

I believe that God uses a vision at times to stretch the believer in their faith. Stretching is important to remove one from their comfort zone. Don't be afraid of being adventurous. I am reminded of the four lepers who were seated outside the gates of Samaria. Within the city, there was a disastrous situation. They were out of food and was selling dove's dung and had come to the place where there was a baby eaten. The four lepers were left with a decision: do we stay here and die? or do we remove ourselves from this place and go toward the enemy? The results were; they left, and it fulfilled a prophecy that was given to the king (see 2 Kings 7:1–20). All of Israel was blessed because someone left their comfort zone.

2. Don't allow the ideas of others to keep you from your vision!

It is important to be convinced that the vision you have is God-given. You cannot allow the thoughts and ideas of others to influence you in making that vision a reality. I know of a pastor that allowed the people to convince him to make a move that was contrary to the vision that God gave him. That church is no longer in existence.

3. You must have an optimistic outlook on your future.

You can see the glass half empty or half full. A pessimistic outlook can stymie you and keep you from progressing in the kingdom. To remain optimistic, it is important to renew your mind daily. The things you dwell on either holds you down or will vault you into your vision. There are times when you will have to deal with criticism. When it occurs, use it as a building block or a stepping stone. When I began in the ministry, my pastor always reminded me that I will encounter those who will give me good advice, and some will give bad advice. He taught me to listen to both and to not throw them away because there are times that even bad advice would be useful, and he was right.

4. **Be selective of the people you hang with.**

The people you are around can play a major role in you obtaining your vision. I once heard it said, "Don't stay where you are tolerated, but go where you are celebrated." In my own experience, I have found this to be true. I believe that Caleb spent a lot of time with Joshua because they both were in agreement with possessing the land of promise. It is vital that you keep company with those that encourage you in the ways of God. Keep hanging with those that tell you, "you can make it." Follow those that are successful in the call that God has placed upon them. Be thankful for those who have been a support system in you obtaining the vision.

Four Elements in Receiving Your Vision

I have discovered four important elements in receiving and accomplishing a God-given vision.

1. **Inspiration.** Webster defines *inspiration* as (1) an inspiring or animating action or influence; (2) something inspired as an idea; (3) a result or inspired activity. Inspiration comes from the word *inspire* which means to fill with an animating, quickening, or exalting influence. To produce or arouse a feeling or thought.

This is one of the first things that happens when a person hears and receives the word of God. When the word comes forth whether it be by preaching, teaching, singing, etc., it brings with it inspiration. Inspiration is the element that births excitement. Remember when the promises of God began to be revealed and the excitement that arose inside of you? That was inspiration at work. This area of inspiration is what I call shouting ground! It is when the believer gets so excited that the shout raises up from within. This is about the time you want to shout, "**Glory to God!**"

Being inspired is an important ingredient in the Christian walk. Without the element of inspiration, it is difficult to move forward in any area of life. Inspiration not only creates excitement, but it gives a sense of being able to accomplish whatever is before you.

2. **Revelation;** Webster defines *revelation* as (1) the act of revealing or disclosing, disclosure; (2) something revealed or disclosed, as of something not before realized; (3) God's disclosure of Himself and His will to His creatures.

Revelation is the unveiling of the Word of God that has been spoken into your life. It is seeing what inspiration has given. It also contains the receiving and understanding of the Word given; it is when the Word becomes alive. So often people try to do what others are doing or saying only to stumble because the Word has yet to come alive within them. The word must come alive personally for you to succeed in your walk with Jesus Christ. When the word becomes alive (revelation received) it enables you to accomplish the will of God.

3. **Illumination;** Webster defines illumination as (1) an act or instance of illuminating, (2) the state of being illuminated. To illuminate is to supply or brighten with a light, to make lucid, to clarify and to enlighten.

Illumination is when the light comes on and you begin to realize what the Word of God is saying. Have you ever read a passage of scripture several times only to read it again, and all of a sudden the light comes on and you have an understanding of what you are reading? That is illumination; it is when the Holy Spirit takes off the veil of your understanding and reveals the spiritual understanding.

Illumination is an important part of our walk with Christ because it opens the truth of the word. When the Word of God is illuminated to you, it brings with it the sense that the Word of God can be applied personally. It brings to reality that you can live in the Word and become what the word is saying about you. Another facet of illumination is it brings to light the ability to become all that the word speaks and to receive the promises of God. It is one thing to get excited about the word and another thing to apply the word. The application of the word is next to impossible without illumination. Illumination is a must for the believer to succeed in his/her spiritual walk and to accomplish the vision.

4. **Application;** Webster defines *application* as (1) the act of putting to a special use or purpose, (2) the use to which something is put.

Inspiration, revelation, and illumination are useless without application. When we hear and understand the Word of God, the responsibility to apply the word is up to us (those that hear and receive). Application is the act of doing what has been revealed. I hear so many Christians say, "*I am trying.*" I stopped trying a long time ago and started doing. The Nike corporation did not become the multibillion dollar operation by saying, "**Just try it.**" No, they said, "**Just do it!**" That is exactly what you and I are required to do with the word that comes alive to us, "**Just do it!**" What good is it to be excited about the word and have an understanding without application. Now with that said, you cannot do it in your own power, strength, and ability. It takes giving yourself over to the direction of the Holy Spirit.

In the Gospel according to Luke in chapter 9 verse 23, Jesus made the statement that whoever comes to Him must deny themselves, take up their cross, and follow Him. The term "*deny himself*" comes with the idea of stop living in our own strength and ability, and allow what Jesus Christ finished at the cross to live in us. We are to walk in the abundant (new life) life that Christ has provided. This can only be accomplished by allowing the Holy Spirit to live in and through us. It is time to apply the knowledge you have gained in your walk with Christ.

When you begin to walk in these elements, you discover that you have become part of your vision. I want to challenge you to never let go of the vision that God has placed within you. Don't allow anything to cloud or remove that vision from you. The vision, that is in you, is an important part of you reaching the plan of God in your life. Continue to reach for it!

* * * * *

Challenge!

Keep a Clear Vision!

Chapter 3

Don't Give into Distractions

"And Caleb stilled the people before Moses, and said, let us go up at once, and possess it. But the men that went up with him said, we be not able to go up against the people; for they are stronger than we." Numbers 13:30–31

Webster defines *distraction* as (1) the act of distracting, (2) the state of being distracted, (3) mental distress or derangement, (4) a person or thing that prevents concentration. Distract is (1) to draw away or divert, as the mind or attention; (2) to disturb or trouble greatly in mind, beset; (3) to provide a pleasant diversion, (4) to separate or divide by dissension or strife, (5) something that interferes with concentration or takes away something else.

If there is one thing that we can agree on, it is that life is filled with distractions. These distractions can come in many forms and diverse areas. We can become distracted by people, places, and things. One can only image the many distractions that tried to get in the way of Caleb and his mountain. When Caleb went into the land of promise and upon his return, he had purposed in his heart that he was going to return to that great land that God had promised. Notice the first distraction that came his way:

* * * * *

Negative Talk

While he was yet speaking and trying to put a stop to negativity, the other men spoke and said, *"We are not able to go up against the people, for they are stronger than we."* They did not stop there; they continued in negative talk. They talked about the giants dwelling there and considered themselves but grasshoppers. I didn't believe that this kind of talk ceased through the forty years that Israel wandered in the wilderness. The scriptures recorded the many murmurings and complaining that went on. It did not matter the many times God blessed them; they continued to find something to complain about. One can only imagine what type of negative talk Caleb heard during his forty-five years of waiting on Mount Hebron.

I can think of a lot of things that can be a distraction, but negative talk has to be at the top of the list. The scripture speaks plainly about how destructive the tongue can be. James said;

> *"Even so the tongue is a little member, and boasteth great things. Behold, how great a matter a little fire kindeleth!"*
> *"And the tongue is a fire, a world of iniquity; so is the tongue among our members, that defileth the whole body, and setteth on fire the course of nature; and it is set on fire of hell. And the tongue is a fire, a world of iniquity; so is the tongue among our members, that defileth the whole body, and setteth on fire the course of nature; and it is set on fire of hell." James 3:5–6*

James continued with the description of the tongue;

> *"But the tongue can no man tame; it is an unruly evil, full of deadly poison." James 3:8*
> *"Out of the same mouth proceeds blessing and cursing. My brethren, these things ought not to be." James 3:10*

Our tongues may be a small member yet a very powerful member. When we speak, it brings some kind of influence, whether positive or negative. Over the period of history, man's tongue has been responsible for a lot tragedy. The tongue has been responsible for a lot of the destruction and iniquity that is in the world today. Negativity from the tongue can bring illness to our bodies. The tongue also makes the path in which we journey in life. The only way to tame the tongue is to give it over to the Holy Spirit.

> *"Death and life are in the power of the tongue:*
> *and they that love it shall eat the fruit thereof."*
> *Proverbs 18:21*

Think about the above scripture for a moment. Within the tongue proceeds life or death. When negative talk continues, the ultimate end is death. It is imperative that we measure what comes from our mouth and what we allow to come into our ears from others. I have always despised it when I hear someone tell a child that they are stupid or dumb. I, like most of you, was brought up by the saying, "sticks and stones may break my bones but words will never harm me." That statement is so far from the truth. Negative talk always has been and continues to be damaging to the ears that hear it.

> *"For by thy words thou shalt be justified,*
> *and by thy words thou shalt be condemned."*
> *(Matthew 12:37)*

Once again, the above passage reveals just how powerful the tongue is. We are either justified or condemned by our speech. It not only affects us, but it also affects those around us. My mother and grandmother always told me that I could do whatever I set my mind to. They spoke positive things into my life, and that was one of the reasons I am where I am today. I don't ever remember being told that I was stupid or dumb even though I did many stupid and dumb things in my life. It is important that we guard what comes from the mouth. I remember one time at work (this was before I turned my life over to Christ); we decided to play a joke on a fellow workman. We started by asking him how he felt. When he answered and said, "okay," we would counter by saying, "are you sure? You don't look so well." After continuing this for a couple of hours, he decided that he didn't feel that good and called a doctor to make an appointment. Words are powerful!

Words that are spoken are not only harmful, but those in print can be just as harmful. If you allow negative words and thoughts to continue to come into your mind, you are faced with a distraction that can become a mountain that would be difficult to climb. I have met a lot of people in the course of my life that are held down because of the words they have allowed in their mind. They become held down by their thinking due to what has been spoken into them.

For forty-five years, Caleb was around negative talk, but he never allowed it to distract him from the mountain he saw in the land of promise. When it came time to receive his inheritance, he said;

> *"As yet I am as strong this day as I was in the day that Moses sent me: as my strength was then, even so is my strength now, for to war, both to go out, and to come in. Now, therefore, give me this mountain." Joshua 14:11–12*

I will discuss this in greater detail in another chapter. But, for now, let's continue on our topic of "*negative talk.*"

Stop allowing negative talk to keep you from your mountain. The talk may continue but you do not have to lend an ear to it. You can and will inhabit your mountain that God has promised! The following are some distractions that try to take your mind off of what God has promised.

* * * * *

People

Another distracter that you encounter is people. Matter of fact, people maybe the greatest distracters of all. Think about it for a moment; how distracting can it be living around a bunch of people who do not say anything good about anything? Life is distracting enough without people adding to it. I have noticed from my own experiences that there is always someone saying you can't make it; you can't do it; etc.

It is often the opinion of people that can be a distraction. I'll never forget the first message that I preached. I was full of fire, very little knowledge, and no wisdom; but I gave it my best. It was about six months later that I was working at the church, and one of the older men in the church was working with me. During our conversation, he told me that when he heard me preach, it was the worst message he had ever heard. My response was, *"I am glad you did not tell me that the night I preached because I may not have ever preached again."* Thank God, it did not distract me from continuing to preach the Word of God and fulfill the calling that God placed in my life. If I had listened to the opinions of others, I would have stopped years ago.

I made mention in an earlier chapter about the two kinds of people that you will encounter in life. But this is a good place to repeat it. You will encounter *"basement people"* and *"balcony people."* The basement people are those who try to pull you down to where they are. They do not celebrate your successes, but will be eager to point out your faults and downfalls. Oftentimes your family and friends can be one of the biggest contributors to this kind of distraction.

The balcony people are those who work hard to pull you up and keep you up. They demand progress and maturity from you. They are the first in line to congratulate and celebrate your success. These are the people that you want to hang with and spend time with. Your time is never wasted by remaining involved with balcony people! Once again I want to remind you to never stay where you are tolerated, but go where you and the gift God has placed within you is celebrated!

* * * * *

Places

Yes, places! You may be asking; what does places have to do with creating a distraction in my life? The truth is; the place where you are at can become a distraction. There are a few things concerning the place where you are; **1.** If the believer does not keep an alertness in their spiritual walk, they can become complacent. Complacency often breeds laziness which can (will) open the door for the enemy to operate. **2.** The surroundings of your place can become a distraction if you allow them to determine how you feel and approach life without the direction of the Holy Spirit. **3.** The believer must avoid getting too content in the place they are. Contentment can get in the way of progressing in the kingdom of God.

The places that I am speaking of are not necessarily geographical. They can be physical, mental, or spiritual. If you have ever been in a place of some kind of physical ailment or living in chronic pain, then you are aware of how distracting it can be. For years, I have lived with chronic pain, and I am aware of how it can be a distraction in one's life.

The mind can be one of those places of distractions and can be one of the toughest to break. The enemy thrives on a person who is mentally unstable. What I mean by being unstable is; when we allow our minds to wander from one thing to another and do not remain focused on the Word of God. The mindset of the believer is so important, so much so that the believer must allow the Holy Spirit to renew their mind on a daily basis. It is important to allow the Holy Spirit the time in giving instructions concerning our mind. In Romans 12:2, we are instructed to "renew" our mind, and that is a daily thing.

In Romans 8:6, we are told that to be carnally minded is death, but to be spiritually minded is life. In 2 Corinthians, the apostle Paul tells us to "cast down" imaginations (arguments) and every high thing that exalts itself against the knowledge of God and to bring into captivity every thought to the obedience of Christ. In Philippians 4:8, we get instruction concerning the things we are to think on, in order to have a clean mind. In James 1:8, we are told that a *"double minded" man* is unstable in all of his ways. With this said, remember that your mind can become a place of distraction.

The place that a person is in concerning their spiritual state can become a distraction. The scripture declares in Romans 8 the problem that arises when one is not in the right spiritual place.

> *"There is therefore now no condemnation to them which are in Christ Jesus, who walk not after the flesh, but after the Spirit." Romans 8:1*

When the believer is living a life walking after the flesh, it leads them to a place of enmity with God, along with a lack of peace in their life! The person who walks after the flesh lives a life of guilt and shame. It can also lead to not mortifying the deeds of the flesh (Ro. 8:13; Col. 3:5) which can lead to destruction. Matter of fact, the ultimate end for those who choose to walk after the flesh is death.

Another distraction is the lack of willingness to change. It is impossible to walk in obedience to the Word and not change. Listening and applying the word brings about a change. Every time I read and study the word, I have noticed that it demands a change in my life. Notice the following scripture;

> *"And be not conformed (fashioned after) to the world: but be ye transformed (changed) by the renewing of your mind, that ye may prove what is that good, and acceptable, and perfect will of God." Romans 12:2*

Understanding the word transformed is extremely important. The same Greek word is used in 2 Corinthians 3:18 where it speaks of being changed. Both of these words come from the Greek word "*metamorphoo*," which denotes a change of condition. The difference in this word and the English word "*metamorphous*" is the latter refers to an external change, to change one's outward form. However, the Greek word "*metamorphoo*" denotes an internal change which is a process in the Christian which takes place or begins to take place upon them receiving Jesus Christ as their Savior (being born again). It is a change of quality not quantity. It is a qualitative change for a new use. This kind of change can only take place by allowing the Holy Spirit to take up residence in our lives.

The lack of a qualitative change becomes a distraction in one's life. The truth is, one cannot follow Christ without this kind of change. It is of great concern for me when I see the so-called believer living a lifestyle of compromise. In the modern-day church, it has become difficult to tell the difference between the Christian and those of the world; this extremely saddens me.

The last distraction (there are certainly more than these) I want to address is our perception. The way we perceive things can become a distraction that does not allow the spiritual progress that is needed in the life of the believer. We must change the way we see things and begin to look through (with) the eyes of the Holy Spirit. I realize that our perception becomes our reality; that is where the danger lies. If the way we perceive something is in reality wrong, we continue to walk the wrong path in life. We need to allow the Holy Spirit to open our eyes that we may see the truth and not fall for a lie.

* * * * *

Things

Things can be one of the greatest distractions of all. It can become so easy to get caught up in the things we have acquired in life. The scriptures talk about a prosperous farmer who had acquired so much in his life that he had to build bigger barns to contain it all. After this he said, "*Soul, thou has much goods laid up for many years; take thine ease, eat, drink, and be merry*" (Luke 12:19–21). His goods had become such a distraction in his life that he missed out on being rich in Christ Jesus and the Cross.

Another story that I am reminded of is one of a "Rich Young Man" who allowed all that he accumulated (his riches) to distract him from following Jesus Christ which led Jesus to say, "*Verily, I say unto you, That a rich man shall hardly enter into the kingdom of heaven"* (Matthew 19:23).

We live in a society where success is often measured by what one has accumulated or possess such as the kind of house we live in, the make of car we drive, the clothes we wear, and the amount of money we have in our bank account. While these things can be a necessity, they are certainly not to be the most important things in a person's life. Neither should they be the measuring reed for success. I personally believe that success is not measured in the things we have but rather the life that we live. When the status quo is based on things, then we have certainly lost sight of what life really is all about. All of the things which we accumulate will one day pass away. The moth and rust will take care of them. However, our spiritual man lives forever, and that should be the most important thing in our life. Living a life following Jesus Christ and His finished work at Calvary is what we really need. We certainly are not able to take our stuff with us when we pass from this life. I heard someone say once, **"You don't see a Brinks truck full of money following the hearse to the cemetery!"**

Gaining stuff (things) in life is not or should not be our top priority. The greatest priority is the way in which we live life and that determines where one spends eternity. We can live serving Jesus Christ who gave Himself for us or we can serve ourselves and be lost. Don't let things be a distraction in your life.

While wandering in the wilderness, Israel allowed Egypt to be a distraction. When things did not go their way they would mention what was in Egypt. It had been said that it took a few days for God to get Israel out of Egypt but a lifetime to get Egypt out of Israel. It is the same way with the believer today. God is still working on us to get the world out of us.

* * * * *

The Challenge!

I have only scratched (if that) the surface concerning distractions that we may face in life. Whatever the distraction may be, I challenge you to be as determined as Caleb was to get your mountain. Remember, distractions are designed to get you off the right course in life, and that course is to live a life of Christ. Whether it is people, words, places, or things, do not allow them to detour you from making progress in your walk with Christ.

One last funny story about myself facing a distraction, I had a particular room that I often prayed in (this was in my early ministry). One day while I was in intense prayer (I thought), there was a mouse that would come out and run around while I was praying. That crazy mouse disrupted my prayer life, so I had to go to a different room to pray in. You talk about a distraction! I hate mice, and to this day, I still do not desire to be in the same room with one!

The way to avoid distractions is;

"Neither give place (position of opportunity) to the devil." Ephesians 4:27 Emphasis Mine

CHAPTER 4

Don't Let Go of the Promise

"These all died in faith, not having received the promises, but having seen them afar off, and were persuaded of them, and embraced them, and confessed that they were strangers and pilgrims on the earth." Hebrews 11:13

Not letting go of his inheritance was another of the great qualities of Caleb that the Holy Spirit revealed to me. It took what I once heard described as "**Bulldog Faith**" to hold onto and refuse to let go of what God promised.

The scriptures are filled with promises to those who dare to believe. The above passage reveals one of the great aspects of faith. Faith has the ability to see what God promises, even when those promises may be in the future. Faith reaches out and embraces them and refuses to let go no matter the surroundings.

The phrase *"these all died in faith"* refers to those believed in the coming of the Messiah, and the deliverance He would bring to all of mankind. The phrase *"not receiving the promises"* relates to the Messiah not coming in their lifetime, yet they continue to hold on to the promises. The phrase *"but having seen them afar off"* refers to the believers that continue to believe even though the promises that they held onto was not yet come. The phrase *"and were persuaded of them"* refers to them holding on to the promises even though they were unseen. The word *"persuaded"* is a strong language when what you are persuaded of is nowhere to be seen, neither anywhere close to where you are at.

When I think about this kind of faith and determination, I am reminded of the great patriarch Abraham who was *"persuaded"* of what God had promised, even though his body was dead and Sarah's womb was unable to carry a child (Romans 4:19–21). The phrase *"embraced them"* indicates that those who believed on the promises refused to let go of them. The phrase *"and confessed that they were strangers and pilgrims on earth."* shows that what they were holding onto was beyond anything that this earth has to offer. Abraham was one of those that believed in what God had promised and Abraham believed that God was able to call things into being.

> ***"As it is written, I have made thee a father of many nations, before Him Whom he believed, even God Who quickens the dead, and calls those things which be not as though they were."***
> **Romans 8:17**

Abraham believed in that which God had spoken in spite of the deadness of his body and Sarah's womb. The truth is (and still remains) when God speaks, nothing has the ability to stand in the way and stop what He has spoken.

In Matthew 16:13–19; When Jesus placed before His disciples the question, *"Whom do men say that I am?"* There were various ideas. But when He approached Peter with his opinion of who He was, Peter's response was, *"Thou art the Christ, the Son of the living God."* Jesus proceeded to tell Peter that His church (the Church that Jesus Christ is the chief cornerstone) was going to be built upon that rock of revelation. He was not calling Peter *"a rock"* as some have taught and believed, but it was the revelation that Peter had concerning who Jesus was. The next statement that Jesus makes is extremely powerful; *"And the gates of hell shall not prevail against it."* This meant that no power would be able to stop what Jesus Christ was going to accomplish at Calvary, and from that great victory, every believer was given the ability to bind on earth what was bound in heaven was and loose on earth what was loosed in heaven. In other words, "nothing will stand in the way of the victory of the cross!"

You may be asking, *"What does this have to do with men like Abraham and Caleb?"* Great question. When God speaks something, it becomes a done deal; nothing is able to stop what God has proclaimed. The men of old (before the cross) held on to that spoken word of God, looking forward to what Jesus Christ was going to do. When Jesus was hanging on the Cross and proclaimed, "it is finished," those three words opened the power of heaven for everyone that would dare to believe. The saints of old relied on what God was going to do, however, the believer of today must live on what Jesus Christ accomplished at Calvary. Jesus spoke it on the Cross when He said, **"It is Finished1"** These three words brought life to all who will believe. Sine He spoke it, we now can walk in the **"Newness of Life"** (Romans 6:1-4).

Just as Jesus spoke it in John 19:30, God spoke it to Abraham (Romans 4:17). Notice, it was God calling those things into existence, not Abraham, but because God called it, we along with Abraham could walk in it. I feel a shout coming on! Excuse me, but I feel a shout coming on!

* * * * *

Against Hope Yet, He Believed in Hope

"Who against hope believed in hope" (Romans 4:18)

With all the odds staked up against Abraham naturally and physically, he yet believed. The word *"hope"* is from the Greek word *"elpis,"* and in Romans 4:18, that word is used twice. First, it was speaking of *"the object of hope, the thing hoped for,"* which means Abraham was hoping for something that seemed impossible, yet he believed in hope. The second word *"hope"* consists of the hope, desire of some good with the expectation of obtaining it. Here, Abraham was still believing against all natural and physical odds with a good expectation of receiving that which God had spoken. Therefore, his hope was not in what he could see or feel but upon what God had spoken. There is nothing impossible with God!

* * * * *

He Was Not Weak in Faith

"And being not weak in faith, he considered not his own body now dead, when he was about a hundred years old, neither yet the deadness of Sarah's womb." Romans 4:19

Abraham refused to look at the outside circumstances that was certainly against him. Abraham did what I call, *"**living from the inside out and not from the outside in.**"* What he did was; he established inside of himself the foundation of what had been spoken to him by God. From this inside foundation of faith, Abraham developed a complete, trust, confidence, and belief on what God said. The key here, for all believers, is not to allow what is seen in the natural get in the way of what the Word of God proclaims. When those negative thoughts and feelings begin to raise up their ugly heads, we (the believer) need to remind ourselves that what God has spoken is more powerful than any circumstances that might come our way.

Jude verse 20 instructs the believer to build up themselves on their most holy faith, praying under the Holy Ghost. Too often we allow what we see on the outside to dictate how we feel on the inside. I know from personal experience that this makes for a miserable way to live. Thank God we can have a firm foundation of faith on the word of God and what Jesus Christ accomplished at Calvary. We must become so strong in our faith in what Jesus Christ finished that nothing, not family, friends nor foes can talk us out of "**Obtaining our Mountain!**"

* * * * *

He Did Not Stagger at the Promises of God

"He staggered not at the promise of God through unbelief; but was strong in faith, giving glory to God." Romans 4:20

Abraham, being strong in faith (having strong faith), allowed him not to stagger at what God had said. It kept him from falling into the arms of unbelief. There are four extremely important things to consider in the above passage:

1. **Abraham refused to waver in faith.** James tells us that a person who wavers is like a wave of the sea that is driven with the wind and tossed. He also refers to that type of person as being double-minded and unstable in all his ways. This person cannot expect to receive anything from God (James 1:6–8). Peter is a great example of one who began his walk on the water and got caught up with the storm surrounding him and began to sink. When Jesus picked him up and they returned to the ship, Jesus said, "*O ye of little faith.*" This term comes from the Greek word "*oliogospistis*" meaning brief, puny, little. Like Peter, many today begin in faith, and it becomes brief because of allowing outside circumstances and situations to interfere with their faith. This is called, "*misplaced faith,*" which means a person's faith is on the wrong object. The believer today, must have the cross and the finished work of Jesus Christ as the object of their faith.
2. **He refused to entertain (stagger in) unbelief.** Unbelief is a direct enemy of faith. Unbelief is from the Greek word

"*apistia*" meaning faithlessness or uncertainty, distrust, unbelief. In the New Testament is used in the sense of:
a) A Lack of knowledge of Jesus Christ (Matthew 13:58; Mark 6:6);
b) Want of confidence in Christ's power (Matthew 17:20; Mark 9:24);
c) In general, it is a want of trust in the God of promises (Romans 4:20; Hebrew 3:12, 19).

Those who entertain unbelief puts themselves in a position to not receive what God has promised.

3. **He was fully persuaded in two very distinct areas:**
   a) He was fully persuaded in what God had promised.
   b) He was fully persuaded in God's ability to do (perform) what He had promised.

   I really like the word *"persuaded,"* it is a compound word consisting of the Greek words *"plao"* and *"plemi"* along with the word *"phoreo"* meaning to fill. Another Greek word that is related to the word *"persuaded"* is *"patristic,"* meaning to fill, to thoroughly accomplish. These together are defined as being established or being brought to an end and completed, reaching its goal; to be proved fully is to be confirmed with the fullest evidence. To be persuaded for the believer is to stand firm on what God has or had promised counting it as already been done and completed. In other words, we don't have to see it in order to know it is a completed promise.

I firmly believed that Caleb possessed the same qualities. We, as believers, must stand firm, being *"fully persuaded"* in what Jesus Christ finished on the Cross (John 19:30). Caleb had waited forty-five years for the promise to manifest. When one takes time to look into those years waiting on a generation of unbelievers to die in order to inherit the land of promise, it is reasonable to consider what Caleb faced. This should be an encouragement to every believer that is waiting on a promise from God. However, that wait can become less painful when one realizes that everything God has promised to us is within the "**Cross and what Jesus Christ accomplished there.**" If Caleb held on (and he did), then we can hold on also.

Think for a moment of what this great man went through and did not allow any of it to interfere with the mountain that he kept in his heart and mind. There was murmuring and complaining all around him continuously. There were those that continually spoke doubt about the promises of God. This is not to mention him waiting on a bunch of doubters to die off so he could receive his "**mountain!**" Remember, everyone above the age of twenty with the exception of Joshua and Caleb had to die before Israel could enter in and possess the land. He was faced with keeping himself from being bitter toward those that were delaying the manifestation of him possessing Mount Hebron. Through all the came against him, he never let go of the promise. Nevertheless, there could have been a distraction for him; after all, it was a distraction to an entire generation.

Whatever promise of God you are holding onto, be encouraged and don't let go. Continue to hold onto the Word of God. For example;

1. You are (were) healed (1 Peter 2:24).
2. You are free from the grip of sin (Romans 6:14).
3. You do have a sound mind (2 Timothy 1:7).
4. You are the head and not the tail (Deuteronomy 28:13).
5. You are more than a conqueror (Romans 8:37).
6. Greater is He that is in you than he that is in the world (1 John 4:4)!

Once the promises of God has been revealed, it becomes the responsibility of the believer to take hold of them and embrace them just as the saints of old (Hebrews 11:13). Keep holding on and embracing what Jesus Christ finished at Calvary and watch those things begin to take hold on your life. The way to embrace and hold onto the promises of God is to keep them in front of you at all times. If you have to, write them down and put them in (on) something that you will be looking at through your day, i.e. a mirror, refrigerator in front of your Bible, etc. Do whatever it takes to keep them on your mind, in your heart, and before your eyes. Just as the woman with the issue of blood reached out and touched (took hold of) the hem (the word) of His (Jesus Christ's) garment and don't let go.

* * * * *

The Challenge!

I don't know how long you have been holding on, but don't give up now. You are closer to the promise than you have ever been. The timeframe for its arrival is irrelevant; just keep holding on. Just as Caleb received his mountain, so will you receive yours!

Chapter 5

Endure Hard Times

"Thou therefore endure hardness, as a good soldier of Jesus Christ." 2 Timothy 2:3

This is another great quality that Caleb possessed. I have seen so many people over the years give up when tough times come. As much as we would like to stay totally away from tough times, they are necessary in building strength. Hard times are also character revealing. They can reveal some of the things that a person needs to work on. James states it well.

"My brethren, count it all joy when ye fall into divers temptations." James 1:2

Here, James is not speaking of the solicitation to sin as he was referring to the trials and tests that the believer faced. This was shown in his next statement;

"Knowing this, that the trying of your faith worketh patience." James 1:3

The testing of the believer's faith helps to develop a strong endurance in the race that is set before him/her. When I was playing basketball, one of the things that I hated most was running those dreadful suicide sprints along with running laps around the gym. What did all of this have to do with playing the game of basketball? It was to develop, expand your lungs and your breathing and also to make stronger legs. I learned early on; the way in which one practiced was often the way one played the game. All of those tough hard practices, exercises, and running drills prepared us for the game ahead.

I have heard it said, *"When tough times come, tough people get going."* John Wooden, who was in my opinion one of the greatest basketball coaches of all time, chimed this great statement; *"Things turn out the best for people who make the best of the way things turn out."* What an awesome truth! It is not the hardship that breaks the person, it is the decision that one makes in the hard times! (Mine)

The term *"endure hardness"* comes from the Greek word *"kakopolos"* this is a compound word, first from *"kakos"* meaning evil and secondly from *"pascho"* meaning to suffer. Together these words mean to suffer evil or afflictions, to be afflicted, to endure, to sustain affliction (2 Timothy 2:9; James 5:13; 2 Timothy 2:3, 4:5).

* * * * *

Facing Hardness

David declared in his thirty-fourth psalm, **_"Many are the afflictions of the righteous: but the Lord delivereth him out of them all." Psalm 34:19_**

The word *"afflictions"* is derived from the Hebrew word *"ra"* which contains several meanings and is determined by the setting and context of the scripture. Here it is described as a wrong, a moral deficiency, mischief, misfortune, adversity, a bad thing that a person does. It is the opposite of good or doing good.

There is not a person that has not faced some kind of hard times. We all have come against some kind of adversity in our walk with Christ. Being a Christian does not exclude one from hard times, however, we are promised victory in those times. I have noticed that hard times often show up when we don't have any control of the situation.

Have you ever had a day when everything imaginable seems to be coming against you? It is also those times when in the natural, a person cannot see any way out. You may even seem to be stuck in quicksand, and you are slowly sinking.

Times of hardness can be a time of separation of the men from the boys. Hard times can reveal those who are in it for the long haul from those that are just playing around. There are stories after stories about people who were faced with hardships and rose above it. They made the best out of a tough situation or a tough environment. I have heard it said, *"Tough times never last, but tough people do."* That statement should come as encouragement when facing hard times. You can make it!

I know from my own personal experiences that victory was often just one step ahead if I would endure tough times. It depends on whether or not you can be tougher than the tough time. I had been in situations where it looked like there was no way that God would come through. Those tough times are character revealing. They have a way of exposing what is within the heart of an individual. I believe tough times make tough people. With that said, I am convinced that no matter how many hard (tough) times are yet in front of us, we can come out victorious.

> *"There hath no temptation taken you but such as is common to man: but God is faithful, who will not suffer you to be tempted above that ye are able; but will with the temptation also make a way to escape, that ye may be able to bear it." 1 Corinthians 10:13*

The apostle Paul was no stranger to hard times. He related some of those times when he suffered hardships:

> *"Of the Jews five times received I forty stripes save one.*

> *Thrice was I beaten with rods, once was I stoned, thrice I suffered shipwreck, a night and a day I have been in the deep;*
>
> *In journeying often, in perils of water, in perils of robbers, in perils by mine own countrymen, in perils by the heathen, in perils in the city, in perils in the wilderness, in perils in the sea, in perils among false brethren;*
>
> *In weariness and painfulness, in watchings often, in hunger and thirst, in fastings often, in cold and nakedness, beside those things that are without, that which cometh upon me daily, the care of all the churches. Who is weak, and I am not weak? who is offended, and I burn not?"* **2 Corinthians 11:24-29**

Every time I read this passage of scripture, what I am facing seems menial in comparison. Paul also mentions the fact that a messenger from Satan was sent to buffet (knock around) him. If there ever was a man who faced intense adverse situations, it certainly was the apostle Paul. Through all of this, Paul was given the answer to his (and ours) coming through all of these hardships. After seeking the Lord three times concerning the thorn in his flesh, God revealed to him (and every believer) the way of escape.

> *"And He said unto me, my grace is sufficient for thee: for my strength is made perfect in weakness."* **2 Corinthians 12:9a**

Upon this great revelation Paul shows his satisfaction by saying:

> *"Most gladly therefore will I rather glory in my infirmities, that the power of Christ may rest upon me."* **2 Corinthians 12:9b**

It is God's grace (His operational power) that is the answer. And that grace (operational power) was revealed by the "***Finished Work of Jesus Christ upon the Cross!***"

* * * * *

Facing a Setback

Hardships can show up in the form of a setback. Some setbacks can be difficult to recover from. When you suffer a setback, you are faced with one of two options: you can sit back, or you can make a comeback. If you have ever been involved in any kind of athletics and suffered a severe injury, you are acquainted with what it takes to make a comeback.

Many years ago, my mother suffered a severe setback when she was in a car accident. She died on the scene and was revived by some great paramedics and was flown by helicopter to a Florida hospital. The doctors did not give us much hope. She had suffered head trauma, and her brain was swelling. Matter of fact, the swelling was so bad that she was barely recognizable. Thank God, He intervened, and she recovered. However, her recovery was long and painful. There were some very simple things that she had to learn to do all over. She had short-term memory loss. She never remembered the accident even until the time she passed many years later. Just settling for sitting back was not in my mother's vocabulary or nature. She took on the mindset to make a comeback.

I remembered a time when I suffered a basketball injury that set me back. It was the first day of practice, and my first trip down the floor I felt something snap in my left groin and my thigh muscle. Two days later, I woke up with huge hematomas from my groin to my knee on my left leg. I had suffered a tendon tear and cracked my pelvis and had a six-inch tear in my thigh muscle. I was on crutches for nine weeks and the therapy was horrible. I had to have a mindset of making a comeback to play ball again. There were literally thousands that have suffered a setback and has never recovered.

Their setback was so devastating that they settled for sitting back. Making a comeback could be a task mentally, physically, financially, and spiritually.

Imagine for a moment and put yourself in the shoes of Joshua and Caleb. They had spent forty days in the land of promise along with ten other men. When they came back from that great land, they all agreed on it being a land of milk and honey. They even brought back a cluster of grapes so large, it took two men to carry it on a staff. I could just imagine the excitement that Caleb was feeling knowing what was in store for him, Mount Hebron. Him and Joshua were primed and ready to go back and walk in their inheritance. They were the only two that brought back a positive report.

The other ten men began to show all of the reasons why they thought the land was unobtainable. Because of doubt, fear, and unbelief of others, Caleb was faced with a setback. It must have been like having a rug pulled out from beneath him. Rather than giving into the negative spirit that was displayed that day, he and Joshua kept their faith and decided to make a comeback. However, that comeback would not come without some challenges. The same is true today. It is not a question of "will setbacks come?" (they are inevitable), but rather, "how will we handle the hardships that setbacks bring?"

You can be encouraged, and know that you can face hardships (setbacks) with the mindset that they are stepping-stones to victory. They (hardships) can pole vault you to your God-given destiny. That is exactly what Caleb did. He used these circumstances as stepping-stones to his inheritance, which was Mount Hebron. I said it earlier but it bears repeating. When you face a set-back, your choices are, sit-back or make a come-back. Those who win in life, are those who decide to make a comeback no matter how devastating the setback. So, don't sit-back make the choice to come-back! Just maybe, we can learn something by how Caleb made his comeback! He used circumstances as stepping stones to his inheritance. I said it earlier, but it bears repeating. When you face a setback, your choices are, sit back or make a comeback. Those who win in life, are those who decide to make a comeback no matter how devastating the setback. When you face a setback, don't sit back, make a comeback!

* * * * *

The Key Is Endurance

Webster defines endurance as (1) the fact and power of bearing pain, hardships, and adversity; (2) the ability to continue or last, stamina; (3) lasting quality; duration. Put in simple terms, it means to hang in there and don't let go or give up.

Caleb's ability to endure hardness began when the word "*nevertheless*" (I call this the spirit of nevertheless) was spoken. While speaking of the greatness of the land came the interruption, and what an interruption it was. When the ten spies used the word "*nevertheless*" it caused excuses to flow as to why they could not overtake and occupy the land. It was a spirit of negativity, and their negative talk spread like a cancer. The following is a list of excuses that came as the result of the "*spirit of nevertheless:*"

1. **The people are strong who live there.**
2. **The cities are walled (fortified) and very great.**
3. **The children of Anak (giants) live there.**
4. **The Amalekites, the Hittites, the Jebusites, the Amorites, and the Canaanites dwell there.**

Caleb had heard enough and he tried to still the people by saying, "*Let's go up at once and possess it: for we are well able to overcome it.*" Then Caleb was interrupted again by the negative talk and mindset of the others. More excuses began to flow from the spirit of nevertheless of the men that went up with Caleb to spy out the land and they brought back an evil report.

5. **We will not be able to go against the people there.**
6. **The people are stronger than us.**

7. **The land eats up the inhabitants thereof.**
8. **All the people we saw were men of great stature.**
9. **We saw giants there.**
10. **And we were in our own sight as grasshoppers, and so we were in their sight.**

A generation of Israel lost out on going into that great land because of the negative language they heard. Not only did they hear it, they bought into it, with the exception of Joshua and Caleb. The spirit of nevertheless always says; "**I would however, I wish I could but, I would like to however, I would if only,**" one excuse after another, and it tied the hands of God for a generation. When you are dealing with this kind of mindset, it can be difficult to rise above it. But thank God, Caleb had another spirit. He had the spirit to endure the hard times that was before him which, allowed him to receive "*his mountain!*"

Once you discover that a negative mindset has taken over, it is important to take action immediately to rid oneself of it. It is made possible by renewing your mind on a daily basis.

> *"And be not conformed to this world: but be ye transformed by the renewing of your mind, that ye may prove what is that good, and acceptable, and perfect, will of God." Romans 12:2*

Without the continuous renewing of the mind, it is impossible to walk with and in the will of God. The mind is the place where most warfare begins. This is the reason behind the scriptures giving instructions to pull down those imaginations that are against the knowledge of God (2 Corinthians 10:4–5). This was a continuous battle for Israel. Matter of fact, I believed it was one of their major problems. Through all of their wandering in the wilderness, they continued to have an Egypt mindset. It seemed that every time they were faced with a difficult situation, they talked about Egypt. It was that mindset that plagued them and caused them trouble.

The time has come that we stop making excuses for not partaking in the promises of God. Not only are the promises of God-given to every believer, but it is His will for every believer to be partakers in them. God is not a respecter of persons, so go after what He has promised (your mountain)!

It is one thing to be wandering in a wilderness place having no idea where you are going. It is important to not allow the wilderness to reside within you. I have often said, "*stop living from the outside in and start living from the inside out!*" What I mean by that statement is stop allowing what is going on around you to dictate what is going on inside of you. This is exactly the position that Caleb was in. I truly believed that he did not allow the wilderness mentality to reside in him and affect him receiving his mountain. The question is; "*How can we survive a wilderness experience without it affecting us in a negative way?*"

First, you must realize that this is only for a season, keeping in mind, this too shall pass. Being in the wilderness can be a time to learn, grow, and gain strength for what lies ahead of you. I have found that it often takes this kind of experience to get one to their destiny. Moses spent forty-years on the backside of the desert preparing him to stand in front of Pharaoh and demand the release of God's people and lead Israel out of Egypt. Jesus was led by the Holy Spirit into a wilderness place. Mathew 4:1. He gave us the secret to overcoming that place. This brings me to point number two.

Secondly, the Word must be in your mouth day and night (Joshua 1:8). The Holy Spirit used that place with Jesus, and it prepared Him to face everything that would come His way. It was proven there (in the wilderness) that Satan could not defeat our Lord and Savior Jesus Christ. Everything that Satan tried to use against Him, Jesus spoke the Word of God.

Thirdly, face the wilderness experience meditating on the Word, day and night. It is important to fill and keep full our minds with the Word of God. It should be in our thoughts at all times. It is the Word that brings victory and removes the wilderness mentality!

Fourthly, you must observe (take a diligent look at) the Word and become a partaker (participating in). The word must be within us, and we must participate in what is written in it to the believers. James proclaimed that we must not just hear the word but be doers of the word. Being a doer of the word is to actively be involved in the word (Joshua 1:8; James 1:22).

Fifthly, you should begin to walk in the success and prosperity of the Word. When we talk about the prosperity and success that the Word brings, we are not talking about becoming a millionaire and owning houses, lands and stuff. I am talking about living in the newness of life that Jesus Christ accomplished on the cross. I am talking about being a participator in the "abundant life" that Jesus spoke of in John 10:10 and which is revealed to us in Romans chapters six and eight.

If you can face your wilderness as a training ground for what is ahead for you, you come out prepared and victorious.

* * * * *

Living Around Grumbling People

I despise being around people who are always grumbling and complaining. These type of people can be some of the most difficult to be around. Have you ever had to spend much time around people who grumble and complain about everything? If your answer is yes, then you know how draining they can be. Have you ever asked someone how they are and they go into about an hour of dissertation and you wished that you had never asked the question? To be around people of that magnitude can be overwhelming. Imagine for a moment; how Caleb must have felt living forty years around a bunch of complainers. Israel complained about everything. When God supplied them with quail, manna, water, and keeping their clothes and shoes from wearing out, they still complained.

Sometimes it can be difficult to separate yourself from this kind of person, especially if they are a member of your household. This reminds me of an old television program called *Hee Haw*. I know. I am showing my age now. On this program, they had a segment with everyone looking sad and gloomy, even, the hound dog. They would sing, *agony and despair on end wooo*. I know people who live that way today. I don't know about you, but I have to remove myself from this kind of atmosphere, and they do create an atmosphere, howbeit gloomy.

If a person is not careful, that kind of mindset and continuing negativity can affect you. This is one of the reasons I admire Caleb so much. He lived around those kind of people, but it never distracted him from the vision of his mountain. Because some have a negative outlook on life, doesn't mean it has to be you nor does it have to affect you. When those thoughts try to bombard your mind, remind yourself what the word of God has promised and what it says about you.

In my years of pastoring, I have heard my share of grumbling and complaining. It was either too hot or too cold. The music was too loud and the sermon was too long. Several years ago, the Holy Spirit spoke to me and said, *"from this day forward if you complain, it will be counted as sin against you!"* My first response was to complain about what was being required of me. After hearing what was required of me (because I knew better), I have had to repent from complaining since then. One thing you don't hear me complain about was the weather. I am a warm (if not a hot) weather person living in Indiana where the winters can be extremely cold. You rarely hear me mention about it being too hot. I might say it is hot but never too hot. Why? Because I was always reminded of how I didn't like (really I hate it) winter. However, I have been trying not to complain about that either because, when it was really cold, I reminded myself, "summer is almost here!"

It is extremely important that we gauge what comes out of our mouths. Words can be damaging. I know as kids we were all told, "sticks and stones make break my bones but words will never harm me." That just simply is not true. Negative words can and often does create negative thoughts, and negative thoughts create a negative heart which create a negative outlook on life. The tongue is a powerful force, so powerful that Jesus said, *"we are either justified or condemned by the words we speak."* (*Matthew 12:37*).

James stated, *"the tongue is a little member, that is a fire that cannot be tamed"* (James 3:5–8). Solomon recorded in Proverbs 18:2, *"the power of life and death are in the tongue."* The only way to get the tongue under control is to have a change of heart, and the way to change the heart is to renew the mind daily. Remember, what you hear gets into your mind and what you think and dwell upon gets into your heart and what gets in your heart eventually comes out of your mouth. Jesus said, *"It is from the abundance of the heart that the mouth speaks"* (Matthew 12:24). This is why we must guard ourselves from allowing negative people to speak negative things into us. I am convinced beyond any shadow of doubt that Caleb did not allow this to be a distraction in his life; he kept his mind on Mount Hebron.

* * * * *

The Challenge!

The next time you begin to feel overwhelmed by your surroundings and what you are going through, get your Bible and read the following passages of scripture:

Begin with 2 Corinthians 11:24–31 and consider what the apostle Paul faced in his ministry. Then read 2 Corinthians 12:1–9 and be reminded of what brought Paul victory. God said, *"My grace is sufficient!"* His grace is also His operational power. It is through the power and grace of God that victory reigns and that grace and power is exemplified at the Cross and what Jesus Christ accomplished there. **"It Is Finished!"** This must be the object of your faith.

Last but certainly not least, sometimes we need to be reminded that God is overseeing everything that is going on in our lives. He is always present no matter how tough things may be so, think on the following:

> *"And we know that all things work together for good to them that love God, to them who are called according to His purpose." Romans 8:28*

The first three words in this scripture, I believe, are the most important, *"and we know."* Without knowing (understanding) that God is in the middle of your current situation and working out good, the rest of the scripture profits you nothing. I am not saying, God is the cause of what is going on (howbeit He can and will try your faith). I am saying, God is involved and working good for you. It gives me strength and courage to know (understand) that God is working on my behalf, and something good is about to happen! God is giving directions to every believer to fulfill His purpose in their lives.

Now that you have discovered that tough times never last but tough people do, you can make it! I live by the following saying, and it has kept me on track and kept me through many hard times and tough situations.

The next time you find yourself facing obstacles of any kind, just step back and let God breath on your situation!

Remember, this too shall pass!

Chapter 6

Don't Lose Your Strength

"As yet I am as strong this day as I was in the day that Moses sent me: as my strength was then, even so is my strength now, for to war, both to go out, and to come in." Joshua 14:11

When the time was growing near for Israel to go and possess Canaan, Moses had passed and Joshua was now the prime leader. Four times God instructed Joshua and all of Israel to be strong. Now forty-five years later at the ripe age of eighty-five, Caleb was ready to get his mountain.

Caleb's statement of strength was incredibly awesome to me, to endure forty years of the wilderness, not to mention his age now. Yet he was as strong as ever. This spoke volumes about his character and faith in what God had promised him through Moses. How many of us can say, after years of endurance, we are as strong as when we started? The truth is, not only should we maintain our strength, but we should have grown even stronger. I imagine that they were few and far between that one could make such a bold statement. However, that should be the result of one's faith walk. It would only be natural to lose some strength over the years. That is if a person is relying totally on his own strength and ability. But here, we are talking about a strength that supersedes any kind of strength that our flesh can provide. The strength that Caleb possessed was the result of his faith and trust in God. He was not relying on his own strength but was standing firm on the strength of God.

The word "*strength*" comes from the Hebrew word "*chazaq*" meaning strong, firm, valiant; sound, powerful, violent, hard. It had the idea of being powerful and having the ability to resist in the sense of violence.

This strength that we were talking about was not necessarily outward but rather an inward strength that supersedes any physical ability. This point was proven when David stood before Goliath. When it came to matching physical strength, there was no comparison. On the other hand, when you look at the inner strength, there was no comparison either. In the physical, Goliath stood far above David while David possessed inner strength that far surpassed Goliath. Caleb walked in this same kind of strength that was provided through faith and trust in God's ability to perform what He had promised.

For the believer today, that kind of strength is provided by the object of their faith being proper, which is in "*the Finished Work of Jesus Christ at Calvary.*" It also comes with the indwelling presence of the Holy Ghost and participating in the word of God. It is through what Jesus Christ accomplished at the cross that allows the believer to stand above all circumstances. The cross is the means, and Jesus Christ is the source of all the believer will ever need.

The apostle Paul said, "*I can do all things through Christ which strengtheneth me*" (Philippians 4:13). The apostle was stating that whether he was in a low place or in a place of abundance, he survives because he draws his strength from Jesus Christ. The word "*Christ*" is from the Greek word "*Christos*" this word has its origin in the word "*Chrio*" meaning to anoint. It was the anointing upon Jesus Christ that enabled Him to endure the Cross and bring victory to all that would (will) believe. That anointing was provided by the Holy Spirit and is available to whosoever. I was convinced that it is through the Baptism in the Holy Ghost and "*the Finished Work of Jesus Christ at the Cross*" (which is first and foremost), that allows the believer to gain their mountain. When the object of our faith is right (as I mentioned before), our walk is right.

In the world of athletics, it is often the athlete that has the greater mental toughness that comes out on top. It is that mental toughness that takes them through the toughest trails and test. I have known of athletes who did not possess the athletic ability as some, but they came out on top because they were tougher mentally. In the spiritual arena, it is those who keep their minds renewed that have an upper hand on the enemy. This kind of tenacity cannot and does not come from the flesh but by the indwelling presence of the Holy Spirit and in what Jesus Christ did at Calvary.

Over the years, I have seen so many people who could never possess the mountain that God had promised them. Some could reach that mountain but could never maintain it. Most of the time, it was a lack of strength and misplaced faith. Just as one must exercise in the natural to gain strength, so is it in the spiritual. We, as believers, must exercise daily in the Spirit. You may be asking, "**How do I exercise in the spiritual?**" Great question. Exercising in the Spirit is done by participating (applying) in the word daily. It is learning to walk in the mechanics and dynamics of the Holy Spirit as is instructed in Romans chapters six and eight. It is through the direction of the Holy Spirit and actively applying and living in the word that brings a spiritual strength to you, the believer.

Several years ago, I used to do a lot of weightlifting and exercising. I would arrive at the gym around 6 am and workout for about three hours. One day during my workouts, a friend approached me and gave me some great advice. He said that he had been watching me workout, and all I was doing was maintenance work. The term was foreign to me at the time. He began to explain to me that the type of exercising and lifting that I was doing was just enough to keep what I had (maintain) strength wise. but not enough to gain muscle and gain strength. What I wasn't doing was pushing myself to do the extra. He began to show me some workout routines that would create more muscle and strength. He called those workouts "**Super Sets**," and man did they hurt and burn. But after a few weeks, the results were well worth the pain and burn. Not only did I gain more strength, but I also began to feel better about myself. There was something about being stronger that created a better self-esteem, while being weak brings a person down.

This reminds me of the condition of many believers. They just do enough to stay saved (if that is possible). What I mean by that statement is that they pray some, read their bible some, study a little, attend church, pay tithe, and they may even volunteer for a church activity; but they never go the extra mile. They do just enough to maintain but not enough to gain. Please understand. I am not talking about works here. I am referring to going the extra mile in your relationship with Jesus Christ. I am talking about your faith and trust being totally given over to what Jesus Christ did at the cross. When a person does just enough to maintain, they are not being totally involved in the Word which is a must in order to possess their mountain (inheritance)! Matter of fact, many of the promises of God continue to elude them. I do not believe that it is the will of God for the believer to just do maintenance work. I believe and am convinced that it is the will of God for every believer to continue progressing and growing in Christ. Again, just doing maintenance work will not cut it. It will take total commitment to the Word and that must be everyday!

In Deuteronomy 28, God gave a promise to Israel that they would be the head and not the tail, and they would be above and not beneath if they would be partakers of His Word! I believe and am convinced that this promise is good for all that believe. Partaking of the Word is a must if one desires to possess their mountain. When the believer begins to walk in the truth of the Word they begin to walk in the strength of God and possess what He has promised. Just as David had the courage and strength to stand before a giant with victory, Caleb had the same ingredients to take and possess Mount Hebron. Caleb had a strength that the rest of Israel did not have. This kind of strength does not come naturally but from the Holy Spirit and our faith being in the right object. God has made this kind of strength available to whosoever.

"Finally, my brethren, be strong in the Lord, and in the power of His might." Ephesians 6:10

Again, when the believer stands in the strength that God provides, they overtake their mountain just as Caleb did. Don't settle for just maintaining strength, but begin to do Supersets in the word and watch your (God's) strength increase in your everyday walk. Not only was Caleb gaining strength, but he was wiser and more knowledgeable concerning the things of God. He was anxious to take that mountain that he claimed forty-five years earlier. Caleb not only possessed the mountain, he ran off the previous owners. It is time to take back all that the enemy has stolen or kept from you. There is a song that we have sang many times over the years, and it has a phrase in it that says, "go to the enemies camp, and take back what he stole from me!"

You might ask yourself, "**What is standing in my way of taking hold on the promises of God?**" I know without a doubt that there is no weapon that is formed against you, the believer, that can be successful. You are also more than a conqueror through the finished work of Jesus Christ at Calvary (Isaiah 54:17; Romans 8:37). The only thing standing in your way of walking in the promises of God is YOU!

* * * * *

The Challenge!

What good is it to take hold of the mountain if you cannot possess it? What good is it to take hold of the mountain and yet not have the ability to maintain it? It is one thing to celebrate a victory but quite another to maintain a victorious attitude. Remember, "*He that is in you is greater than he that is in the world*" (1 John 4:4).

NOW, GO AND POSSESS YOUR MOUNTAIN!

Chapter 7

Remain Courageous

"Have not I commanded thee? Be strong and of a good courage, be not afraid, neither be thou dismayed: for the Lord thy God is with thee withersoever thou goest." Joshua 1:9

The word "*courage*" is mentioned four times in the first chapter of Joshua in the KJV. Strong's Complete Dictionary of Bible words defines "*courage*" as coming from the Greek word "*amats*" the prime root is to be alert in courage. To confirm, be courageous (of good courage, steadfastly minded, strong, stronger), established, fortify, harden, increase, prevail, strengthen (self) make strong. Webster defines the word "*courage*" as; the quality of the mind or spirit that enables a person to face difficulty, danger, pain, etc. without fear, bravery.

From the above description, the person who possesses courage is one who has a made up mind to walk in strength with the thought of prevailing over the enemy. It is a quality of the mind that enables that person to face a diversity of battles. This kind of mindset can come only by the believer to continually renew their thinking (Romans 12:2). This kind of courage is shown through the person who continues to move forward in spite of all the fearful things that may surround them. It is being courageous in any given situation.

When I think of a person who possesses the characteristic of courage, I think of a soldier on the battlefield. I have talked to many decorated veterans of war, and they have said in the moment of their valor they did what they did in spite of fear that may have surrounded them. Sometimes being courageous is being brave beyond fear. I believe that this is a quality that every child of God should possess. The truth is courage comes with the infilling of the Holy Spirit. Too often many of us spend time trying to remove fear rather than moving forward in spite of fear. When this happens, that person loses the battle, and they lose the opportunity to walk in victory. I am convinced that one of the greatest slap to the face of the enemy is when that same person continues to pursue in battle, in the middle of fear.

Fear can be the greatest distraction of someone being courageous. The secret is when fear surrounds you, don't allow it to effect the courage that is within you. As I have mentioned before, courageous people are those who continue in battle when fear is all around them. I believe that courage is the direct result of the faith that is within the believer. Fear is the greatest enemy to faith, however, the scripture declares,

"For God has not given us the spirit of fear; but of power, and of love, and of a sound mind." 2 Timothy 1:7

Notice, that fear is a spirit, a negative spirit at best. When looking at the above passage of scripture, there is a wealth of information for the believer. **First**, the phrase *"God has not given us the spirit of fear"* reveals to us the mind set that the Holy Spirit brings to the believer. Paul was actually telling young Timothy not to fear or be afraid of the those who may or will oppose him. **Secondly**, the phrase *"but of power"* this refers to the power and might of the indwelling Holy Spirit. **Thirdly**, the phrase *"of love"* refers to the presence of the Holy Spirit, for it is only through Him that the believer can walk in the true spirit of love. **Fourthly**, the phrase *"and of a sound mind"* the Holy Spirit brings with Him the ability for the believer to have a soundness of mind which is also known as *"the spirit of self-control."*

When the believer walks in the power, love, and the soundness of mind under the direction of the Holy Spirit, they walk in faith and not in fear.

When you look at the report of Caleb, he never said that there was a fear factor when spying out the land of Canaan. I am sure that the presence of giants brought fear; the other ten spies related that fact. I am also sure that the walls of Jericho were overwhelming. However, Caleb never once showed any kind of fear. Matter of fact, Caleb said, **"We are well able, let us go up at once and take possession of the land."** This is the displaying of the attitude of courage that every believer should be walking in. This world is full of fear factors, but through Jesus Christ, we are overcomers of the world (John 16:33).

I can remember when I was in the army; we were put into some training situations, and fear was surrounding us, but we did our job in spite of the surroundings. The same thing can happen, and often does, in our spiritual walk. Not every step we take and not every place we go may be fear free. However, that is when true courage comes to the surface, and we continue on no matter what is happening in the natural world. True courage comes from within; it is the strength that is supplied to the believer by the Holy Spirit.

Being courageous is revealed in our faithfulness to Jesus Christ. As I mentioned earlier in this chapter, the call for courage, (being courageous) is mentioned four times in the first chapter of Joshua. Israel was instructed to not be afraid of what was before them but to be of good courage. Joshua was calling for the people to be full of faith and not fear when entering into the land of promise. They were to be full of faith no matter what they heard or saw. This call was to relieve them of any fear that may try to overtake them. When the ten spies began to spew their negative report, (*"there are giants in the land, there are walled cities, there are great nations mightier than us, and we are but grasshoppers in our own sight"*); fear spread like wild fire in the hearts of Israel. Giving in to the negative report in spite of the courage of Caleb, there was a generation who was not allowed to partake in the promises of God.

I believe that same call is going out to believers today. It is a call to be courageous! It takes a courage that far surpasses anything that the flesh can supply, in order for the believer to walk in victory and receive their mountain. When you think about the courage displayed by many of those before us, it should be of great encouragement to all believers to remain in the walk of faith.

> *"Wherefore seeing we also are compassed about with so great a cloud of witnesses, let us lay aside every weight, and the sin which doth so easily beset us, and let us run with patience the race that is set before us."*
>
> *"Looking unto Jesus the author and finisher of our (the) faith; who for the joy that was set before Him endured the cross, despising the shame, and is set down at the right hand of the throne of God."* Hebrews 12:1–2 Emphasis Mine

When I think of people of great courage, I think of those that are listed in the eleventh chapter of Hebrews, known as the "*Hall of fame in faith*." These are great witnesses to courage one to walk in faith. Here are some examples:

1. **Abraham, who left his own country to answer the call of God (Genesis 12)**
2. **Joseph, who became the "Viceroy" of Egypt (Genesis 41:37–45)**
3. **Moses standing before pharaoh (Exodus 7)**
4. **Rahab letting down the scarlet cord (Joshua 2: 12–16)**
5. **David standing before and slaying Goliath (1 Samuel 17)**
6. **The three Hebrew boys in the fiery furnace (Daniel 3:19–28)**
7. **Daniel in the lion's den (Daniel 6:16–22)**

And these are just a few, for the list of witnesses goes on and on. Surely, if these could make it through the adversities they faced, you and I can make it through what we are facing now. I realize that there are times when facing certain adverse circumstances, they can seem overwhelming, to say the least. Sometimes just everyday living can takes its toll on the believer. I can remember hearing some of my elders (when I was a child) saying, when they were facing a difficult situation, *"You just have to pick yourself up by the bootstraps!"* Well, while that maybe some great advice, it often seems easier said than done. This is where I believe that courage has to come on the scene. Forget about the circumstance that is before you and allow courage to rise from within you and face every situation knowing you come through with victory, possessing your mountain. When you do this, you discover yourself growing in courage and before you know it the mountain is yours. You will obtain the promise of God. This reminds me of the following story:

"The Race"

"QUIT! GIVE UP! YOU'RE BEATEN!" They shout out and plead, There's just too much against you now, this time you can't succeed. And as I start to hang my head in front of failure's face, my downward fall is broken by the memory of a race.

And hope refills my weakened will as I recall that scene. For just the thought of that short race rejuvenates my being. A children's race, young boys, young men; now I remember well. Excitement, sure, but also fear; it wasn't hard to tell.

They all lined up so full of hope. Each thought to win that race or tie for first, or if not that, at least second place. And fathers watched from off the side, each cheering for his son. And each boy hoped to show his dad that he would be the one.

The whistle blew and off they went, young hearts and hope of fire. To win, to be the hero there, was each boy's desire. And one boy in particular, his dad was in the crowd. Was running near the lead and thought, "My Dad will be so proud."

But as he speeded down the field across a shallow dip. The little boy who thought to win, lost his step and slipped. Trying hard to catch himself, his hands flew out to brace, And mid the laughter of the crowd, he fell flat on his face.

So down he fell and with him hope. He couldn't win it now. Embarrassed, sad, he only wished to disappear somehow. But as he fell his dad stood up and showed his anxious face, Which to the boy so clearly said, "Get up and win that race!"

He quickly arose, no damage done—behind a bit, that's all, And ran with all his mind and might to make up for the fall. So anxious to restore himself to catch up and to win, His mind went faster than his legs. He slipped and fell again.

He wished that he had quit before with only one disgrace. I'm hopeless as a runner now, I shouldn't try to race. But, in the laughing crowd he searched and found his father's face That steady look that said again, "Get up and win the race."

So, he jumped up to try again. Ten yards behind the last. If I'm to gain those yards, he thought, I've got to run real fast. Exceeding everything he had, he regained eight or ten, But trying so hard to catch the lead, he slipped and fell again.

Defeat! He lay there silently, a tear dropped from his eye. There's no sense running any more—three strikes I'm out— why try? The will to rise had disappeared, all hope had fled away. So far behind, so error prone, closer all the way.

*I've lost, so what's the use, he thought! I'll live with my disgrace.
But then he thought about his dad, who soon he'd have to face.
"Get up," an echo sounded low, "Get up and take your place.
You were not meant for failure here, get up and win the race."*

*With borrowed will, "Get up," it said, "You haven't lost at
all, For winning is not more than this: To rise each time you
fall." So he rose up to win once more. And a new commit,
He resolved that win or lose, at least he wouldn't quit.*

*They cheered the winning runner as he crossed first place.
Head high and proud and happy; no falling, no disgrace.
But when the fallen youngster crossed the line, last place, The
crowd gave him the greater cheer for finishing the race.*

*And even though he came in last, with head bowed low,
unproud, You would thought he had won, to listen to the crowd.
And to his Dad he sadly said, "I didn't do so well." "To me
you won," his father said, "You rose each time you fell."*

*And when things seem dark and hard and difficult to face,
The memory of that little boy—helps me in my race. For
all life is like that race, with ups and downs and all, And
all you have to do to win is rise each time you fall.*

*"QUIT! GIVE UP! YOU'RE BEATEN!"
They still shout in my face. But another voice within me says,
"GET UP AND WIN THE RACE!"*

—Author unknown

When I read the above story, it brings to mind a passage of scripture that is dear to me. I cannot count the times that the following scripture has ministered to me and gave me strength to continue in my faith walk.

> *"Be not deceived God is not mocked: for whatsoever a man soweth, that shall he also reap.*
> *"For he that soweth to his flesh shall of the flesh reap corruption: but he that soweth to the Spirit shall of the Spirit reap life everlasting."*
> *"And let us not grow weary in well doing: for in due season we shall reap, if we faint not."*
> **Galatians 6:7–9**

Within this passage of scripture there is a wealth of information that every believer must heed to if, they desire to walk in a life of victory. Let's examine this passage phrase by phrase and receive the revelation that is within it.

The phrase *"Be not deceived"* reveals to us a two-fold meaning. **1.** It is possible for a believer to be deceived if they fall prey to false teaching. False teaching is anything that says there is another way to salvation. **2.** The believer can be deceived when the teaching removes our faith from what Jesus Christ finished at the cross, which must be the focus of every believer.

The phrase *"God is not mocked"* refers to the fact that what God has said will come to pass and nothing will ever change that. To stop preaching the cross (the cross is the means) and all of its benefits that Jesus Christ accomplished there (Jesus Christ is our source) is a mockery to God.

The phrase *"For whatsoever a man sows that shall he also reap,"* brings to light the law of reciprocity, which is the law of sowing and reaping. Everything that God created, He gave the ability to give after its own kind. That is why dogs do not give birth to kittens, and horses to not give birth to calves, etc. You and I can be sure that what we sow in our life is exactly what we reap and nothing will ever change that.

The phrase *"For he that soweth to his flesh shall of the flesh reap corruption,"* this pertains to the person who is trying to live according to their own ability, strength and knowledge rather than depending on Jesus Christ and has their faith in something other than what

Jesus Christ did at Calvary, see Luke 9:23. The flesh will always produce corruption, and will ultimately lead to death, see Romans 8.

The phrase *"But he that soweth to the Spirit,"* this reveals living a life that is directed by the Holy Spirit which brings a newness of life to the believer, see Romans chapters six and eight. It also pertains to a person who will put all of their trust and faith in the "**Finished work of Jesus Christ**" which was accomplished at Calvary.

The phrase *Shall of the Spirit reap life everlasting,"* this goes back to a statement that Jesus made in John 10:10b, *"I have come that they might have life, and that they might have it more abundantly,"* The more abundant life is revealed in Romans chapter six. It is, as I mentioned before, the ability given to those who dare to believe and have faith in what Jesus Christ has done for us. It is not believing in what God can and will do but believing and trusting in what Jesus Christ has already done.

The phrase *"And let us not grow weary in well doing,"* this should be the goal and attitude for every believer and it is accomplished when we continue to live (sow) in the guidance of the Holy Spirit.

The word *"weary"* comes from the Greek word *"ekkakeo"* which denotes cowardice, faintheartedness; to be unfortunate, to be desperate. It is vital that the believer guards against becoming a coward (afraid to move forward), or to be overtaken by the spirit of desperation. When we set out to accomplish and live in what God has set before us, it is not time to shrink back. When a person becomes desperate, it often leads to a tragic ending. Nothing good ever comes from shrinking to cowardice and desperation.

The word *"well"* comes from the Greek word *"kalso"* which is defined as constitutionally good without necessarily being benevolent. It comes with the idea of remaining in agreement with the word of God, in all that one does or says.

The word *"doing"* comes from the Greek word *"poleo"* meaning quality. It denotes the quality of work that qualifies for a harvest. In other words, when you examine the harvest you see the results of the quality of time and effort that is put into your work. The work that I am speaking of is the work that is produced as the results of your faith. The right kind of faith always produces the right kind of works.

Works never produces faith, however, true faith produces true works (see James 2:14–22).

Let me give you an example of what I am referring to. Where we used to live, we were surrounded by farm land. The land was farmed by two different farmers. One year, they both planted beans. In one field, the beans never did get above my knees, while in the other field the beans grew well above my waist. What made the difference? One farmer had installed a watering system and the other didn't. One went the extra mile, while the other didn't. I'll let you decide who had the better crop. This same rule holds true in our spiritual lives. It is the quality of your faith that produces the right work which produces a great harvest!

The phrase "*for in due season we shall reap*" the timing for your (our) harvest is within the hands of God. It is God who determines the season in which we reap our harvest. With that being said, I am convinced that when our (your) faith is in the right object (**Jesus Christ and the Cross**), it brings the harvest quickly and abundantly.

The phrase "*if we faint not*" is referring to remaining in the right kind of faith and not substituting it for our own ability (again see Luke 9:23). If we are to not faint, we must deny ourselves from living according to our ability and begin to trust wholeheartedly in what Jesus Christ has accomplished for everyone who believes. Then we must take up our cross, which is the victory side of the cross and follow Christ. This means that we as a believer have come to the conclusion that it is all about what Jesus Christ did and not what we can do.

When we put this passage of scripture in proper context, it gives instruction to every believer to keep up the good work; don't become desperate, and stay in continuous agreement with the word. Along with being courageous and keeping up the quality of your faith, which is walking in "**the faith**." Once you come to this place, you can watch God reward you with a great over-abundant harvest!

The apostle Paul told us of just how he (and we should) lived his life.

> *"I am crucified with Christ: nevertheless, I live; yet not I, but Christ liveth in me: and the life which I now live in the flesh I live by the faith of the Son of God, who loved me, and gave Himself for me." Galatians 2:20*

Did you notice how Paul said that he lived his life? It was by "**the faith**" of the Son of God, Jesus Christ. The term "**the faith**" is referring to what Jesus Christ accomplished at Calvary. Paul lived his life by the faithfulness of Jesus Christ and put all of his faith and trust in the finished work of Christ. I realized that I have repeated this a lot in this chapter. My reasoning is due to the modern-day message that is excluding the cross of Christ. One man wrote and taught that if we continue to preach the cross, we are preaching death. That would be funny if it wasn't so far from the truth. Paul said in 1 Corinthians 1:17, 18, 23 that preaching the cross of Christ, His crucifixion and resurrection, is the gospel.

The apostle Paul continued in verse 21 of Galatians 2 saying, "*I do not frustrate the grace of God.*" When we put our faith in anything other than the finished work of Christ, we are frustrating the grace of God, which means we nullify and put a stop to how God works, which is by grace. Paul found that out when God told him that His grace was sufficient for him (2 Corinthians 12:9).

*****

The Challenge!

Remain faithful and be of good courage. Keep your focus on what Jesus Christ has accomplished for you. Now, go forth and take your mountain!

Chapter 8

Don't Throw Away Your Confidence!

"Cast not away therefore your confidence, which hath great recompense of reward."
Hebrews 10:35

Confidence was another great quality that was displayed by Caleb. Along with his great courage came a confidence that allowed him to continually stand firm in his faith. The word *"confidence"* in this passage pertaining to being courageous, to take a firm bold stance. It also consists of a bold manner of speaking. Notice in Hebrews 10:23:

"Let us hold fast the profession of our faith without wavering for He is faithful Who promised."

The apostle Paul, here, was speaking of holding fast to what Jesus Christ accomplished at Calvary. This was the place and the only place where the believer should have their faith. Let's take a closer look at this scripture and how it relates to *"not casting away our (your) confidence."*

The phrase *"Let us hold fast"* comes from the Greek word *"kat-echo."* This is a compound word *"kata"* and the word *"echo"* together they have the idea; to have, hold, hold fast in a spiritual sense. It also comes with the idea of taking possession, to seize, to possess. In this sense, it would be taking possession of what one's faith was centered upon.

The word "*profession*" is from the Greek word "*homologia*" which is related to the word "*homologeo*" meaning to say the same thing. It is a confession, profession, and recognition of Christ being the chief Priest of our confession. This means that, as a believer, our speech, manner of speaking should come in agreement with Christ and His finished work. It is being in agreement with the fact and truth of who Jesus Christ is and what He finished at the cross.

The phrase "*of our faith*" is from the Greek word "*elpis*" which means, hope, desire of some good with the expectation of obtaining it. It is the object of hope, the thing hoped for (Romans 8:24; Hebrews 6:18; Galatians 5:5; Colossians 1:5; Titus 2:13; Hebrews 7:19). It is the foundation or ground of hope. It is having confidence and security in someone, of course this is speaking of Jesus Christ and His finished work at Calvary.

The phrase "*without wavering*" comes with the idea of standing firm and not allowing anything to detour you away from our great high priest, Jesus Christ. The believer can take this kind of stance with the assurance of what Jesus Christ promised you (the believer) can possess, obtain, and walk therein.

This is exciting to me, for when you put this altogether, it reveals that we can have confidence in what Jesus Christ has said (promised) and what He has done (the cross)! After digging into verse twenty-three, it brings verse thirty-five alive!

I really like the way the Amplified Bible reads these two scriptures:

> ***"So let us seize and hold fast and retain without wavering the hope we cherish and confess and our acknowledgement of it, for He Who promised is reliable (sure) and faithful to His word." Hebrews 10:23***

> *"Do not, therefore, fling away your fearless confidence, for it carries a great and glorious compensation of reward." Hebrews 10:35*

This is exactly what Caleb did in the process of obtaining his mountain. Whatever it is that God has promised, you can go to the bank with it. He does what He said. As believers, we can go forward, agreeing in our actions and speech with what the Word of God proclaims.

I believe that this gives great clarity as to why and how Caleb was able to withstand the roadblocks that tried to keep him from obtaining and living in what was promised! He lived these forty-five years in agreement with the promises of God! When Caleb first saw this mountain forty-five years ago, it was known as **"Kirjah-arba;"** the city of four giants (the Anakims). It was named after Arba, who was the greatest of those giants. Caleb was not detoured because of the inhabitants of this great mountain. He, at no time, showed fear of the giants who lived there! **(Joshua 14:10-12)**. Caleb walked in **Divine Faith,** which is a faith that conquers all enemies!

When Caleb took possession of **"Kirjah-arba"** it became known as **Mount Hebron,** which means **"fellowship!"** It is fellowship with God! Where you find this kind of **Faith**, you also find **rest from the war!**

When I think about Caleb, and how he came against Arba, it reminds me of another great warrior who stood his ground against a giant! David was but a lad when he came up against the greatest warrior of the Philistines: a giant of a man named Goliath. This great warrior stood well over nine feet and weighed over six hundred pounds. He was not only huge, but was a well trained fighter. He stood on the mountainside, challenging anyone from the camp of Israel to fight. When you consider the size and lack of warfare experience of David, he was no match for such a champion! However, he did not face Goliath in his own strength and ability: he came with the power and authority of the **Lord God of Israel!**

"Then said David to the Philistine, You come to me with a sword, and a spear, and with a shield: but I come to you in the Name of the Lord of Hosts, the God of the armies of Israel, Whom you have defiled." 1 Samuel 17:45 NKJV

There are a diversity of things that are doing whatever possible to keep you, the believer, from obtaining your mountain. Just as David stood before Goliath and as Caleb stood for forty-five years, we (the believers) must stand with a firm confidence knowing beyond any doubt that God is not only able but through Jesus Christ and His finished work has already done (accomplished) the victory for you. Your mountain is standing there waiting on you to take possession. When your faith is in what Jesus Christ has already done nothing can keep you from what He has promised but you!

The enemy does everything he can to keep you from that mountain that God has promised. He throws everything at you (the believer), he can get his hands on. One of his greatest weapons is fear. If the enemy can dictate any kind of fear, he will use everything in his arsenal to stop you. This is called, "**FACING YOUR GIANT**." I learned a long time ago that some people can talk a good fight, but when you begin to look in their eyes, if any fear is within them, it shows. I am here to tell you, within the eyes of Satan, is a fear of you and I walking in total confidence in what was accomplished at the cross of Calvary. He fears that you gain a bold manner of speaking and agreeing with the truth of the word of God!

We are all faced with some kind of obstacle here and there. Those obstacles from the enemy are designed to stand between the believer and the manifestation of what God has promised. I have learned in my walk of faith that nothing comes easy. However, I have also learned that anything worth having is worth fighting for. As a believer, you must make up your mind; is this mountain (promise) worth fighting for? The kind of warfare that every believer faces is certainly not for the fainthearted. But the good news is *"He that is in you, is greater than he that is in the world!"* (1 John 4:4).

Remember earlier when we gave the definition of the term *"profession of our faith"* and that coming from the Greek words *"homologia and homologeo"* meaning, saying the same thing, coming in agreement with the Word. I am convinced; this is an area where a lot of believers come short. When I listen to the way some believers talk, it leaves little doubt to why they are in the shape they are in. Jesus spoke something that I believe is of a great importance to every believer but often gets glossed over. Notice what He said in the following passage of scriptures.

> *"Either the tree good, and his fruit good; or else make the tree corrupt, and his fruit corrupt: for them a tree is known by his fruit."*
>
> *"O generations of vipers, how can ye, being evil speak good things? For out of the abundance of the heart the mouth speaketh."*
>
> *"A good man out of the good treasure of the heart bringeth forth good things: and an evil man out of the evil treasure bringeth forth evil things."*
>
> *"But I say unto you, that every idle word that men speak they shall give account therefore in the day of judgment."*
>
> *"For by thy words thou shalt be justified, and by thy words thou shalt be condemned."*
> *Matthew 12:33–37*

The above passage is full of revelation. Jesus had been accused by the Pharisees as casting out demon spirits by the power of Beelzebub, the prince of devils. Which, by the way, was totally ludicrous. Jesus began teaching about a house being divided. He stated that if Satan was casting out demons, his (Satan's) house would be divided and his kingdom could not stand. Either Jesus was right, or the Pharisees were. Jesus in His teaching began to use the analogy of a tree and the fruit that comes from that tree.

It just makes good sense that a tree cannot bear good and evil fruit at the same time. Notice in verse thirty-three. Jesus said, *"Either make the tree good, and his fruit good or make the tree corrupt, and his fruit corrupt."* The question is, "How can a person make the fruit of the tree good or corrupt?" Jesus gave clarity to that very question. The fruit that the tree produces is the result of what is within the heart of the individual. It is within the heart where you can find the treasure of a person. Notice. Jesus said, *"It is out of the abundance of the heart that words come from our mouth!"* It really doesn't take long to understand what a person believes and what kind of outlook they have in life, just listen to them speak. Solomon also makes a powerful statement concerning that manner in which one speaks.

> ***"Death and life are in the power of the tongue: and they who love it shall eat the fruit thereof."***
> ***Proverbs 18:21***

When the believer (or any person) continually speak words of doubt, fear, and unbelief, they are speaking words that lead to death. I know of some people that all they talk about is their (as if they own it) sickness all of the time. I despise to be around people who continue in negative talk. Have you ever asked someone how they are doing, and an hour later, you wished that you had never asked the question? Being around negative talk breeds negative thinking, which results in negative speaking. And according to the writer of Proverbs, which is the Holy Spirit, bad talk leads to bad results.

On the other hand, speaking words that are in agreement with the Word of God brings life. This is where the term *"homologia and homologeo"* come into the picture. Remember in Hebrews 10:23, where the term *"profession of our faith"* is used? Your tree is known by your profession, that which is flowing from your mouth.

In our culture today, I hear so many people say, "**You are judging me.**" There is a huge difference in passing judgment on someone and discerning what kind of fruit they are bearing. I know very little about how to tell the difference in some trees, however, when it comes fruit bearing time, I have no problem telling one tree from another. Stop and think about it for a moment. It is not difficult to tell what tree you are of; we just have to listen to your manner of speaking. I am convinced that Caleb continually was speaking about his mountain during those waiting years. I don't believe for a minute that he allowed anything negative to come from his lips concerning what God had promised.

What God has promised the believer should be a part of your speaking through out each day. In order for that to happen, you must, and I put emphasis on the word must, get the word of God deep down within your heart, then and only then does it begin to flow from your mouth. Remember, *"from the abundance of the heart the mouth speaks."* And your mouth only speaks of what the treasure is in your heart. Your treasure is the result of what you want in your life. Your fruit is only as good as what is within you.

Some people are good at what I call "**surface speaking**," however, they eventually reveal what is in the deep recesses of their heart. So, whatever you do, keep the word of God within your heart and mouth and watch what begins to come your way!

* * * * *

The Challenge!

**Read and study the Word every day!
Make room for the Word of God in your heart!
Make your manner of speaking to agree with the Word!**

"Thy word have I hid in mine heart, That I might not sin against thee." Psalm 119:11

CHAPTER 9

Do Not Waver in Your Faith

"But ye, beloved, building up yourselves on your most holy faith, praying in the Holy Ghost." Jude verse 20

I mentioned in an earlier chapter concerning not allowing yourself to waver in your faith. In this chapter, I want to examine it in a little different perspective. The foundation for every believer must be "their faith." Without faith, there is no direction; neither is there anything to reach for. Not to mention that without faith, it is impossible to please God. The scriptures also proclaim that whatsoever is done, it must be done in faith or it is sin (Hebrews 11:6; Romans 14:23). Just from these two passages the, importance of faith and having its right object rings loud.

It is within the faith of the believer that gets them through life. When the believer's faith is in the right object (Jesus Christ and what He did at the Cross), it brings them into a life of victory. That victory is obtaining all that Christ did and living in the newness of life (see Romans chapter 6). The key is to be able to keep the faith in the middle of all kinds of adversity. When we read Hebrews chapter eleven, we discover not only the faith of the believer's but also the adversity they faced. It is when they stared adversity in the face and continue in the faith, that victory come to them.

Have you ever noticed, when you decide to make a stand in the faith, that adversity swiftly make its way to you? Well, that is not by accident. That should tell us that there is an enemy warring against anyone and everyone that gets involved in the faith walk. Once you make a firm stand, it sends a red flag to the enemy, saying it is time to attack. The apostle Paul made this abundantly clear in the following statement,

> *"I have fought a good fight, I have finished my course, I have kept the faith." 2 Timothy 4:7*

Let's take a moment here and examine further what Paul was saying. First, he declared he *"fought,"* this means that he was engaged in a warfare to contend for the victory. This word generally indicates to fight or wrestle. It also comes with having the faith to be able to persevere in the face of trials and temptations. The importance of this is the *"perseverance"* that every believer must have in order to arrive at the destiny that God has designed for them. The fight that every believer finds themselves in, comes from an unseen source.

> *"For we wrestle not against flesh and blood, but against principalities, against powers, against the rulers of the darkness of this world, against spiritual wickedness (wicked spirits) in high places." Ephesians 6:12 Emphasis Mine*

Paul continued in verse fourteen and told the believer to *"stand."* What this all means is; it is time we (you) as believers *"stand our (your) ground."* If you want your promised mountain you have to continue to stand.

Secondly, Paul said that he fought a *"good fight."* The word *"good"* comes from a Greek word that means, completeness, balanced and proportioned. It also indicates a lawful fight, which means Paul fought the fight within the Word of God! If you are going to obtain your mountain, then you must fight the enemy with the Word of God. The word *"fight"* implies force or violence. The apostle Paul often used these words in regards to the Greek games, where many athletes would compete for a crown in their particular field. If you have ever been involved in any kind of sporting event, then you can understand why the apostle used this kind of language. When a person is competing at any level, there is a demand that is placed upon him/her to perform at their very best. This demand involves sacrificing from the athlete. Their body and mind must be in tip-top shape.

Notice the two words *"good fight"* that there is a balance and proportion to the believers fight. This comes by practice after practice and persevering through pain and even injury. This allows the athlete to compete at his/her best. I can remember when I was heavily involved in athletics; the practice time was not always great. But, it taught me endurance and perseverance. I also found the way in which one practices is the way they ultimately perform. The same is true for those who are living the faith life. Just as you can count on adversity showing its ugly head, you can also be sure that faith sees you through any adverse circumstances.

There are a lot of things in this life that you cannot put your trust in. Have you ever trusted in the word of someone, only to be let down? I am sure that you have experienced that a time or two. When I was child growing up on a farm in Indiana, I witnessed my grandfather enter into a promise, contract, covenant, or whatever you choose to call it, with nothing more than a handshake. Once those two hands came together in agreement the deal was sealed. You could count on each party to come through on their promise. Times have certainly changed over the last sixty years. It is sad to say, but too often the words of people do not mean what they used to. Of course, I am not saying that this applies to everybody, however, it applies to many. This brings up the question, "**Is there anybody we can go to and trust what they say?**" The answer to that question is a resounding, "**Yes!**" You can stand firm on what the Word of God proclaims. God's word is unchangeable, and the connection between the believer and what God has spoken is their faith. It is faith that brings into manifestation the promises in the word. Faith in the correct object never lets you down. Faith takes you to new levels and dimensions in the kingdom of God. We discuss this in a later chapter. You can count on the faith. Matter of fact, I mentioned earlier in this chapter, faith must be the foundation for the believer to mature and build on. That is faith in the finished work of Jesus Christ (see Hebrews 11:1; Hebrews 12:2).

* * * * *

Do Not Misplace Your Faith

If it is true that the faith never lets the believer down, then what is the problem? The problem is most of us at one time or another has let faith down. What I mean by that statement is; there are times when we may have started out in faith, only to allow something else to get in the way of our journey. Jesus addressed this problem on at least four different occasions. In each of these, He used the term, "*O ye of little faith.*" Let's examine them.

1. **The anxiety of needs being met.** In these passages, Jesus addressed the issue of anxiety (worry) concerning what a person is going to eat, how they are going to be clothed, and where are they going to live. His instruction to them was, "*But seek ye first, the kingdom of God, and His righteousness and all these things will be added to you.*" (Matthew 6:30; Luke 12:28; Matthew 6:33).
2. **The fear of harm or accident** (Matthew 8:26). In this passage, the disciples were in a ship. A storm arose and fear gripped their hearts. They awoke Jesus saying they were perishing. Jesus spoke to the wind and the sea and a calm came. He then responded to them saying, "*O ye of little faith.*"
3. **When facing fear and doubt** (Matthew 14:31). This is the story of the disciples being put in a ship and Jesus telling them that He would meet them on the other side. A tremendous storm came upon them, and the disciples saw what they thought was a spirit walking on the water. Jesus

knowing that fear had gripped their heart said to them, "*Be not afraid; it is I.*" Then Peter responded saying, "*Lord if it be you tell me to come unto you*" (emphasis mine). Jesus said, "*Come!*" It was at that moment, Peter got out of the boat and began to walk on the water. Somewhere during his walking on the water, he took his eyes off of Jesus and began to concentrate on the storm. Beginning to sink he cried out to Jesus for help. Jesus lifted him up, and they went back to the boat. Once again Jesus used the phrase, "*O ye of little faith.*"

4. **The forgetting of previous blessings** (Matthew 16:8). The disciples had just left from seeing the miracle of the feeding of four thousand, and that was not counting the women and children. Jesus had taken seven loaves and a few little fishes and fed the multitude. Everyone there are until they were full, and there remained seven baskets filled with leftovers. When the disciples had come to the other side, they had forgotten to take bread. They were confused when Jesus was talking about being aware of the leaven of the Pharisees and Sadducees. They reasoned among themselves, that Jesus said this because they had not brought any bread. How soon some of us forget what God has performed for us in times past. Even if Jesus was speaking about natural bread (He is the bread of life), He could have supplied that just as He supplied the fishes and loaves to the multitude. Once again, Jesus used the phrase, "*O ye of little faith.*"

The term "*O ye of little faith*" comes from the Greek word "*Oligopistos*;" this is a compound word "*oligos*" meaning; little, small, brief or puny, "*pistos*" meaning,: believing faith. When we combine these two words, it is defined as little faith, trusting too little, insufficient faith, brief or puny faith, or lacking confidence in Christ.

In each of these cases, there is a common thread. They all begin their particular journey in faith, then due to surrounding circumstances, they lost sight of the object of their faith. Their walk in faith was small, brief, and puny at best. They gave up giving attention to the things around them which caused them to enter into doubt and or fear. Once you waver in faith, you have left faith at that moment. This is critical because, the scriptures proclaimed that anyone who wavers cannot expect to receive anything from God.

> *"But let him ask in faith, nothing wavering. For he that wavereth is like a wave of the sea driven with the wind and tossed. Let not that man think he shall receive anything of the Lord. A double minded man is unstable in all his ways." James 1:6–8*

It is a continuous fight to hold onto the faith. The enemy likes nothing better than to see the believer give up in the middle of the battle. Part of the battle is not letting go of the faith. As I stated earlier, the apostle Paul fought a good fight, and he kept the faith. He did not allow outside circumstances to dictate what he believed or how he felt inside. His faith was as simple as God said it, therefore, I believe it. He placed all of his faith in **"The Finished Work of Jesus Christ at Calvary!"**

With all the surroundings that Caleb endured, with the opportunities that were before him to give up, he never let go of his faith. That was a key for him, as well as it is for every believer in obtaining their mountain (inheritance). Caleb was strong in his faith. He counted God faithful, and he remained faithful to God he was so strong in his faith that nothing nor anybody could talk him out of living by faith and obtaining the promises of God. Once again the apostle Paul puts it into perspective:

> *"I am crucified with Christ, nevertheless I live; yet not I, but Christ liveth in me: and the life which I now live in the flesh I live by the faith of the Son of God, who loved me, and gave Himself for me." Galatians 2:20*

The above scripture is one of my favorites. It is filled with revelation that is life changing. I want to focus on one statement that Paul makes; *"the life that I now live in the flesh I live by the faith of the Son of God."*

What makes this statement so important is how Paul said he lived his life. Notice, it was by the faith of the Son of God! Simply put, Paul revealed that his life was ongoing because of *"the faith"* (the faithfulness) of Jesus Christ. When Paul used the term *the faith*, he is referring to what Jesus Christ accomplished at the cross. In other words, Paul's faith was in what Jesus Christ had already done. Paul became faithful because of the faithfulness of Jesus Christ the Son of God! The object of Paul's faith was in the cross and what Jesus Christ did there. This should be (must be) the way that every believer lives their life. We (the believer) should be so strong in our faith concerning what Jesus Christ has already done and not allow outside situations remove us from the faith. We (the believer) can't just quit just because times get a little rough. There is one thing you and I can be sure of in this life, things do not always go the way we want them to. But, if we remain faithful to God and keep our eyes on the prize, we can run this race that is set before us and finish in victory.

Too often, I have witnessed people waver and let go of faith, right at the point of their breakthrough. If you take time to read and study Hebrews chapter eleven, you find that those who remained and continued in the faith received what God had made available to them.

* * * * *

The Challenge!

Just like Caleb, you too have an inheritance. It is God's will and desire for you to obtain and walk in that inheritance. Keep in mind; there is an enemy that tries everything he can to hinder and prevent you from obtaining your "**Mountain.**" He tries to put things in your path to stymie your growth and progress in God's kingdom. The key to receiving all that God has is to "**NEVER LET GO OF THE FAITH!**"

CHAPTER 10

Stretch Your Faith

The Difference in the Ordinary and the Extraordinary

"but the people that do know their God shall be strong and do exploits." Daniel 11:32b

In this chapter, I want to deal with the differences between those who want from those who have. There is a difference in being ordinary and being extraordinary. As we get started, let's look into the above scripture and examine the statement of Daniel.

"The people that do know their God," The word *"know"* in this passage is deeper than a simple knowledge concerning the existence of God. It means to be in a personal intimate relationship with God. There are untold millions of people who recognize the existence of God but are not intimately involved with God.

The term *"shall be strong"* refers to those you are no longer walking in their own strength but are totally relying on the strength of God to live their everyday life. Paul relates this message to those in Ephesus when he said,

"Finally, my brethren, be strong in the Lord, and in the power of His might." Ephesians 6:10

The term "*do exploits,*" this comes with the idea of doing the extraordinary, strange, out of the ordinary, creating a breakthrough.

The Amplified Bible reads this way, "*but the people who know their God shall prove themselves strong and shall stand firm and do exploits* [for God]."

The believer is not called to just be ordinary and or settle for the ordinary. Jesus said the things that He did we shall do also.

> *"Verily, verily, I say unto you, He that believeth on me, the works that I do shall he do also; and greater works than these shall he do; because I go unto my Father." John 14:12*

The apostle Peter referred to the believers as

> *"But ye are a chosen generation, a royal priesthood, a holy nation, a peculiar people; that ye should show forth the praises of Him who hath called you out of darkness into His marvelous light." 1 Peter 2:9*

The word "*peculiar*" jumps out at me every time I read this passage of scripture. It comes from the Greek word "*els*" this word is used often to indicate, intention, purpose, identity, aim.

It also has with it the idea of being purchased as a people of purpose. Some believers have never came to the knowledge that they were purchased by Jesus Christ at Calvary, not to just make heaven their eternal home, but to make a difference in this life.

From here, I want to examine the difference between the "*ordinary*" and the "*extraordinary.*" The word "*ordinary*" is defined as the customary, the usual, regular, normal, to be familiar, unexceptional, common. Relatively poor or inferior. The word "*extraordinary*" is defined as not according to the usual custom or regular plan; going far beyond the ordinary degree or measure or limit, etc.; very unusual, exceptional.

You may be asking the question, **"What is wrong with being ordinary or average?"** After all, average is the usual or normal thing.

"**So, what is wrong with that?**" I like the way John Maxwell answers these questions.

"Average has been described as, **the top of the bottom or the best of the worst and the worst of the best!**"

Did you get that? **(1) the top of the bottom, (2) the best of the worst, (3) the worst of the best!** I believe and am convinced that God has set apart the believer from the world, and we are to be above the ordinary. There was nothing about the things that Jesus Christ did that was the usual, the regular, or the norm in this world. What He did was in the realm of the extraordinary. It was not like the world for He was not of this world and neither are you and I as believers (John 8:23; 15:19; 17:14,16). Jesus went further to declare that His kingdom was not of this world.

What separates the average from the above average? What is it that separates those who want it from those who have it? What separates those who dream a dream from those who live the dream? What separates those who can from those that do? What separates those who won't from those who will? What separates those who talk it from those that walk it? What separates those who hear from those that do what they hear? The following are some things that reveal how the average (ordinary) is separated from the above average (extraordinary).

1. *Sight;* they see what they can have not just what they have. One says, "**I have to see it in order to believe it.**" Another says, "**I believe it therefore, I see it.**" The above average see what they can be in Christ, and their sight is not limited to what they are presently. They focus on the solution, not the problem. While the average (pessimist) see the glass half empty, the above average (the optimist) sees the glass half full. This is extremely important because our perception becomes our reality. The way we see things is of the utmost importance. Ask yourself the following:

   How do I see myself?
   How do I see the things around me?

Do you see yourself as a victim or a victor?

Can you see beyond your current situation and see yourself healed?

2. *Their talk is different.* One tells it like it is according to their surroundings. Another tells it like it can be or will be according to the promises of God. While one is being overwhelmed by their surroundings and complain, the other one says, "It is well!" The above average believer has their talk in alignment and agreement with the word of God. Several years ago, the Lord spoke to me in my complaining state and told me that from that day forward, my complaining would be counted as sin. Yes, I have had to ask for forgiveness. Every now and then, I catch myself complaining or about to complain. I am not saying that if you complain, it is sin to you, but it is for me. The above average does not talk doubt and unbelief.

3. *Their walk is different.* They continue to walk in the ways of the word against all odds. They walk in the "Grace of God" (His operational power). They deny themselves and pick up their cross and follow Jesus Christ. What I mean by that statement is; they stop walking in their own power, strength, and ability and begin to walk in the strength and ability that was supplied to them from what Jesus Christ did at the cross, His finished work. They walk with the cross of Christ as their object of faith. They walk in the newness of life that Christ has purchased. (Luke 9:23; Romans 6:4).

4. *They are people of change.* What I am referring to here is; when the word of God is revealed to them, they take the necessary steps to conform to the word and not the world (see Romans 12:1–2).

5. *The people they hang with.* They hang with those who encourages them and teach them the Word of God. They hang with the people who will pull them up when they fall. These are the "*Balcony People*" that I have spoke of earlier.

These are the people that will encourage and be of great help in you obtaining your mountain. A great example to this is the man with palsy and his friends that took him to Jesus for his healing. They also hang with people who celebrate them and not just tolerate them.

6. *They do not allow obstacles to stop them from progressing.* The above average (the extraordinary), use obstacles as stepping-stones to success.
7. *They are participators, not spectators.* They participate in the word. So many people hear the word and say amen but fail to participate in what they heard.

* * * * *

They Stretch Their Faith!

Another separation from the ordinary and the extraordinary is their faith. The extraordinary stretches themselves in the faith. The following are a few examples:

1. **They build their boat before it rains.** When Noah heard the voice of God instructing him to build an Ark, he did not hesitate nor did he wait for the first rain drop to make sure he heard from God (see Gen. 6:9–22).
2. **They go before they know.** Abraham who was from the land of Ur of the Chaldees among strange gods heard God speak, "Now the Lord had said unto Abram. *Get thee out of thy country, and from thy kindred, and from thy father's house, unto a land that I will show thee.*" (Genesis 12:1). Abram did not have any idea where he was going nor what his destiny was at the time. However, he left his country of strange gods and wholly followed the Lord. Over the years of ministry, I have noticed something about God. A person can be at point "**A**" and God will speak and say, "**Go to point B**" and that would be the extent of the command. I

used to wander why God did not reveal the journey. Well, for one, if we knew all the details of the journey, most of us would never start. Then again if we knew all the details, it would no doubt cause fear to rise up in us. Last, if we knew all we would not need faith for the journey. So, the next time God speaks to you, don't hesitate or spend time fleecing, get up, and go as God directs. The Holy Spirit leads the way.

3. **They fight through fear and get out of the boat.** Peter has received so much criticism for sinking while walking on the water. However, out of all that was in the boat, he was the only one to get out when Jesus said, "*Come.*" He walked on the water, and when fear arose, he cried out to Jesus, and I believe that he and Jesus walked on the water back to the boat. Don't allow fright to keep you from being obedient to the word of God. Stretch your faith and get out of the boat of your own reasoning.

The scriptures are full of individuals who stretched themselves in the faith. Hebrews 12 begins by saying, "*Wherefore seeing also are compassed about with so great a cloud of witnesses.*" Read chapter eleven and you will see and hear from that great cloud of witnesses. They faced the unknown, left their own country, was tried by fire, faced giants and lions. Many faced obstacles with courage that only faith can birth.

* * * * *

They Expand Their Horizons

It is not God's intention for you to stay where you are. He has new horizons for you to explore. There is lying before you, an opportunity to get to the next level (I am not talking necessarily geographical but spiritual). The following are some things you encounter and also some things you must do to expand your horizons and get to the next level.

You Must Become A Line Crosser!

1. **Cross the line of the unknown**; crossing this line takes you into new territory. It is a place where you have never been. It can be a place that you have only dreamed of. In order to cross this line, there must be a change in your thinking. Too often the way a person thinks can keep them from the unknown. It was the mindset of the ten spies that kept Israel from entering into the promised land. However, the right way of thinking can open up a new life for those that dare to believe. The following are some examples:

"By faith Abraham, when he was called to go out into a place which he should after receive for an in-heritance, obeyed; and he went out, not knowing whither he went." Hebrews 11:8

It was by faith in the words of the prophet Elijah that a widow sustained him. When he told her to make him a cake first and God would cause her meal barrel to never waste, she obeyed, and her meal barrel was not wasted. (1 Kings 17:8–16).

There are many more recorded in scripture that obeyed the word of the Lord and found themselves crossing the line into the unknown. If you are a person who must know all the details before you begin your journey, you can never be the one who crosses this line. The Swiss watch company was presented with the opportunity to make the Quartz watch. They passed because they did not believe it would sell. Timex took the chance and crossed the line of the unknown, and the rest is history! Don't be afraid to be a line crosser.

2. **Cross the line of the impossible**; this is what I call, "miracle territory." It is here where you must strip yourself of

doubt and unbelief. This is when you take a few loaves and fishes and feed a multitude! Charles Haddon Spurgeon once wrote, "***God delights in the impossibilities.***" One man says, "***I will do as much as I can.***" He says, "**any fool can do that; He that believes in Christ Jesus does what he cannot do, attempts the impossible, and performs it**, **for Jesus said, 'If you have faith as a grain of mustard seed nothing shall be impossible to you!'"**

Crossing this line is when you do not have the natural ability to accomplish what needs to be done. Yet you make the move to do it! This is when one must rely totally on God's ability to work through them. It is where you transform trouble into triumph. You make the impossible, possible and the invisible, visible through the power of the Holy Spirit that resides within you! (Romans 4:13–21; Hebrews 11:11–12).

3. **Crossing the line of sacrifice**; this is the place where one must stop relying on their own strength, and ability. It is where you must deny yourself and wholly follow Christ. Luke 9:23. In order to cross this line, you have to make a stand against negative feedback. It is where you have to examine yourself to see if there is anything hindering you from advancing in the kingdom of God. In this place, the will of God will be revealed (see 2 Corinthians 13:5; Romans 12:1–2).
4. **Resist the pull to return**; throughout the history of Israel, there was always present the pull to return to Egypt. This was especially true when times get tough. (Hebrews 11:15). For the believer now, it is the pull to rely on the flesh to see them through. There are always those who try to get you (the believer) to go back to the good old days.
5. **Cross the line of tradition**; those who remain stuck in tradition like to live in the way that they always did things. Their thinking concerning trying something new can be, "*this will never work,*" or "*we have never done it this way*

before." The future seems to scare them. This reminds me of a story I heard many years ago; in preparing for a dinner, the mother was going to cook a ham. She cut the ham in half and placed it into two separate pans. Her young daughter was watching carefully and asked her mother, *"Why did you cut the ham in half?"* The mother replied, *"I don't know; that was the way your grandmother always did it. You will have to ask her, why?"* The young girl asked her grandmother who answered her saying, *"This is the way my mother, your great-grandmother, always did it. You will have to ask her as to why."* When the young girl asked her great grandmother, she was surprised at her answer. Great-grandmother said, *"I don't know why your mother and grandmother are doing it that way, but I did it that way because I did not have a pan large enough for the whole ham!"* Now, that explains tradition! The church world is filled with it, and it can stop the believer from progressing to performing the will of God.

In order to become a line crosser, you must be a person of faith, Your trust must be in what Jesus Christ did at Calvary. You must also be a person of sacrifice. You need to relinquish the desires of your flesh and conform to the will of God (see Psalm 37:4). You must become a person of patience, not allowing frustration to set in while on your way to the goal that is before you. Use any failures or setbacks as stepping-stones.

* * * * *

What Drives the Ordinary to Do the Extraordinary?

1. **Their Love for God**—they possess such a love for God and for what He has called them to do. Let me use myself for an example (not being boastful); I don't serve God just to miss hell and the lake of fire. I serve the Lord not only for what He did at Calvary, but I serve Him because I love

Him. I have been a student of the Word for many years now, and that is because I love the word of God and have a deep desire for an understanding. I have been in the ministry for many years now, and I love it as much if not more than when I started. I did not go when God said go, for the money, fame, or fortune. I went because I love God and the gospel of Jesus Christ. I want to bring this great gospel to all that will hear. I am driven by love!

2. **Their Faith**—they are persuaded beyond any doubt concerning the promises of God. They are convinced in the ability of God to perform His Word. Most of all, they have their faith in the cross and what Jesus Christ finished there. They have made "**The Faith**" their foundation. (John 19:30; Jude 1:20).

3. **Their Determination**—great people are ordinary people with an extraordinary amount of determination. They keep getting up when they fall down. When they suffer a setback, they don't sit back; they make a comeback. Their determination is the result of their dedication and commitment to Jesus Christ.

* * * * *

The Challenge!

How Much Do You Want?
How Deep Do You Want To Dig?
How Much Are You Willing To Give Of Yourself?
Begin to Increase Your Love For God!
Begin to Stretch Yourself in the Faith!
Get More Determined In Your Walk With Christ!

Chapter 11

Delays Do Not Mean No!

"To everything there is a season, and a time to every purpose under the heaven." Ecclesiastes 3:1

There are times when it seems as though God has forgotten to perform what He promised. It isn't that God has forgotten, it is often not the right time or season. I call them "*delays.*" Before we get too involved in the delays, let's first look at the above passage of scripture and look deeper into three important statements that are made:

1. **There is a Certain Season.** This term is from the Hebrew word "*zman,*" this is a noun and only occurs three times in the Old Testament and is derived from the word "*zaman,*" meaning to be appointed, to be determined, to be fixed. It means appointed time or times. Sometimes it may seem as if God is delaying the manifestation of His promise, however, most of the time, it is due to it not being the season for it to take place. We will explain this in greater detail later in this chapter.
2. **And a Time**, the word "*time*" in this passage is from the Hebrew word "*eth*" meaning time, the right time, the proper time. There are three principle situations which the word describes: (1) regular events, (2) the appropriate time

for an un-recurring incident, and (3) a set time. Only God knows when the time is just right and appropriate.
3. **Every Purpose**, the word *"purpose"* is from the Hebrew word *"chephets"* meaning to find pleasure in, take delight in, be pleased with; it also signifies, pleasure, delight, wish, desire. The season and the time for the believer is to fulfill God's purpose in their life. There can be many reason why there seems to be delays in our lives. Let's look at some examples in the scriptures where there seems to be delays in what God promised.

Noah is a great example. From the time that God spoke to Noah in Genesis 6:13–14, there was a span of about ninety-eight years before the flood began in Genesis 7. There was a lot of work that had to be done in that timeframe. I am convinced that Noah did not know the day nor the hour in which the rain would begin. However, he worked diligently to perform what God had commanded him to do. I once heard it said concerning the return of Jesus Christ that "we should work as if it could be a thousand years but live like He is coming back at any moment."

Abraham is another person who persevered through a delay. When God spoke to Abram in Genesis chapter twelve promising him, that in him, all the families of the Earth would be blessed. He was about one hundred years old before the promise began to unfold in the birth of Isaac. During this delay, there were a lot of things that Abram went through until the birth of Isaac. He and Sarai went through a name change from Abram to Abraham and from Sarai to Sarah. God waited until physically Abraham nor Sarah could not have any children, then God showed up! Those years were really not delays; they were a time of preparation.

From the time that Caleb received the promise of his inheritance, forty-five years passed before he took possession of his mountain. One can only imagine some of the things that he endured. I am sure those forty-five years seemed like an eternity of delays before he obtained what was promised to him. However, he said that he was as strong now and as capable of war as he was forty-five years ago. That lets me know that Caleb used that time to grow in faith and trust in the Lord. He kept that mountain before him!

David is another individual who seemed to face what one could consider, delays. David was about fifteen years old when he was anointed by the prophet Samuel. David was thirty years old when he began his reign over all of Israel, and he reigned for forty years. He reigned over Judah for seven years and six months and in Jerusalem for thirty-three years. I do not have the time nor space in this book to go into all that David faced while he was waiting for his anointing to be king. All of those years when it looked as if there were delays, it was actually a time of training and development for David.

You may be thinking, *"Why is it taking so long for the promises of God to come forth?"* Don't look at it as God is delaying but God is preparing you for what is ahead of you. When I look back at my forty-eight years of being in the ministry, I can now see where God was preparing me each stage of my life. There were times when I thought God was delaying this or that, only to discover that God was waiting on me. He was waiting on my development in the Spirit in order to place me at the right place at the right time. There is nothing that I can think of that brings misery like being at the wrong place at the wrong time. I don't know about you, but I have been there, and it was not enjoyable.

There are seasons of preparation as I mentioned earlier. Some seasons last longer than others. I do believe that God has appointed seasons and set times for certain things. I am convinced that if there are many delays, it is because we (maybe I should just speak for myself) are lagging behind, or there is more need for improvement.

* * * * *

Wait Upon the Lord

"But they that wait upon the Lord shall renew their strength; they shall mount up with wings

as eagles; they shall run, and not be weary; and they shall walk, and not faint." Isaiah 40:31

The above scripture is a favorite for many believers. Let's take an exegetical look at what the prophet Isaiah said. The term *"they that wait"* comes from the Hebrew word *"qawah"* meaning to bind together (by twisting); to be joined together, be joined; to meet; to lie in wait for someone; to expect, await, look for patiently, hope; to be confident, trust, to be enduring (another kind of strength).

The term *"upon the Lord"* reveals what the focus of every believer must be. To take that a step further today, it consists of the believer having as their object of faith, **The Cross and the Finished Work of Jesus Christ**. So, to say, *"they that wait upon the Lord,"* is to say; they take time to bind together and join together with the Lord, with an expectation, hope and confidence in what He accomplished at Calvary. While waiting upon the Lord, the believer is constantly seeking to do His will.

The word *"renew"* actually means *"to change."* So, they wait upon the Lord shall *"change"* their strength. This comes with the idea of no longer relying on one's personal, physical strength, but to live in the strength of the Lord. Jesus made a statement recorded in the Gospel according to Luke, that often gets overlooked or *"If any man will come after Me, Let him deny himself, and take up his cross daily and follow Me."* **(Luke 9:23).** I have heard this scripture literally butchered over the years. Let's take a closer look at what Jesus said. *"If any man will come after me,"* this statement is speaking to all those who come to Jesus Christ for salvation. Upon this statement, Jesus lays down the criteria for the believer. (1) "Let him *deny himself.*" I love what Jesus said here. His statement calls for every believer to stop working and living in their own strength and ability. It is a call to enter into a rest that only comes through and by what Jesus Christ did at the cross. It is actually a call to exchange our own physical strength for His strength. Then He continued by saying, *"take up his cross daily."* Notice the cross in which Jesus was speaking here is the **"believer's cross!"** There are actually two elements to the cross. The *"suffering side"* and the other side is the *"victory side."* Every believer is to walk in the benefits of the *"victory"* that Jesus Christ accomplished there, and we are to do it daily following Him!

Jesus Christ made it possible for you and I to exchange our strengths for His, and when we do, we then can, *"mount up with wings as eagles!"* The term *"mount up"* comes from the Hebrew word, *"alah,"* meaning to ascend, mount up, go up, rise, to grow up, to be lifted up, put up, to be led up, to be high, be exalted. The example of being like eagles is certainly no mistake nor is it a play on words. The eagle is set apart from all other birds; it is full of beauty, and even though they grow old, they can take on the appearance of forever being young. As believers, we have been given the promise that if our faith is focused on the correct object, *the Cross and what Jesus accomplished there*, we can exchange our strength for His and travel the journey that is set before us and not be weary or faint!

* * * * *

Be Patient

"But let patience have her perfect work, that ye may be perfect and entire wanting nothing."
James 1:4

While we are facing those times when it seems like there is a delay in reaching our destiny, the above passage of scripture gives some solid advice. The word *"patience"* is from the Greek word *"hupomone,"* which is a compound word, *"hupo,"* meaning under; and *meno*, meaning to abide. This comes with the idea of showing patience, endurance as to things or circumstances. It is long-suffering, endurance, with people. *"Hupomone"* also is associated with hope (1 Thessalonians 1:3) and refers to the quality that does not surrender to circumstances or succumb under trial. This brings with it the idea that the believer should never surrender nor give up while facing any trial, test or delays.

The word *"perfect"* comes from the Greek word *"telelos,"* meaning complete and reaching the goal and or purpose. The word *"work"* is from the Greek word *"ergon,"* meaning performance, the result or object of employment. It denotes any matter or thing, any object which one may have to do or obtain. It generally denotes acts by which the man proves his genuineness and his faith. So, the perfect work of patience brings the believer to a place to obtain what Jesus Christ did at Calvary. It makes the believer complete, entire (matured) and wanting nothing! **(James 1:4)**.

The word *"entire"* is from the Geek word *"holokleros"* which is a compound word, *"holos,"* meaning all, the whole; and the word, *"kleros,"* meaning a part, share. Together, *"holokleros"* denotes, whole, having all its parts, being sound, and perfect (fully matured). Also, retaining all that is allotted (By the Finished Work of Jesus Christ) which makes the believer wanting nothing for their completeness; bodily, mental and moral entireness.

The next time you feel like you are in a state of delay, take the opportunity to bind together with Jesus Christ, and allow the entire complete work of patience take place within you. I was inspired by the Holy Spirit in writing this book due to seeing so many Christians struggling in their faith walk. Often times our walk of faith can be a great challenge. If the promises of God seem to be eluding you and if it appears that at the point of a breakthrough you suffer a set-back, this is a must read. The Holy Spirit gave me a tremendous revelation concerning a man named Caleb. It was forty-five years after Caleb first looked upon the promise of God (the land that flowed with milk and honey). Within these pages you will discover the many characteristics of this great man that kept holding onto and pursuing what God had promised. When applying these revealed principles in your everyday life, you too can take possession of the **"Mountain"** (inheritance) that God promised!

*****

The Challenge!

Hang in There When Delays Come!
Take Every Opportunity to Grow and Mature!
Take Time to Bind Together with the Lord Jesus Christ!
Mount Up with the Wings of Eagles
And Soar in the Person of the Holy Spirit!
Do not grow weary nor faint hearted in your journey!

Chapter 12

It Is Finished

"Looking unto Jesus, the author and finisher of our faith; who for the joy that was set before Him Endured the cross, despising the shame and is set down at the right hand of the Throne of God." Hebrews 12:2

In the previous chapters we have shared the different characteristics of Caleb that kept him in pursuit of his inheritance. It was forty-five years after he first saw Mount Hebron that Caleb uttered the words, "**Give Me This Mountain**." Mount Hebron was called "**Kirjath-arba**" the city of Arba. Arba was a great man among the Anakims who were giants. It was the tenacity of Caleb's faith in God and His promise of a "**Land that would flow with milk and honey**," after his wait of forty-five years and the time of receiving his inheritance Caleb proclaimed,

"And now, behold, the Lord hath kept me alive, as He said, these forty and five years, even since the Lord spake this Word unto Moses, while the children of Israel wandered in the wilderness: and now, lo, I am this day fourscore and five years old."

> *"As yet I am as strong this day as I was in the day that Moses sent me: as my strength was then, even so is my strength now, for war, both to go out, and to come in."*
>
> *"Now therefore give me this mountain wherefore the Lord spoke in that day; the Anakims were there, and that the cities were great and fenced: if so be the Lord will be with me, then I shall be able to drive them out, as the Lord said."*
>
> *"And Joshua blessed him, and gave Caleb the son of Jephunneh Hebron for an inheritance." Joshua 14:10–13*

The strength of Caleb was totally due to his faith in God. While Israel wandered in the wilderness (with a wilderness mindset), Caleb's mind was stayed upon the Lord and his inheritance. Upon overtaking the inhabitants of Hebron (Kirath-arba), the land rested from war.

While all of those listed in the **"Hall of Fame of Faith"** looked forward, to the promises of God and not receiving them, they yet could see them afar off and was persuaded of them (Hebrews 11:13). However, today's believer is to look from a different perspective, he/she are to **"Look Back."** That is, to **"Look back at the Cross and what Jesus Christ accomplished there."** In our introductive scripture (Hebrews 12:2), the believer is instructed to, *"Look unto Jesus, the author (beginner) and finisher (it was finished at the Cross) of our faith."* By this statement, I am not suggesting that the believer today does not have anything to look forward too. There are yet a lot of great things that are yet ahead of us. In the Revelation, that was given to John while on the Isle of Patmos; the believer has a promise ahead of them.

> ***"He that overcometh shall inherit all these things*** (The only way and I stress, the only way one can become and overcomer is to put all his/

> her faith in, "***The Finished Work of Jesus Christ and What He accomplished at the Cross***") ***and I will be his God, and he shall be My son***, (Upon receiving Christ as one's personal Lord and Savior we become part of the Family of God.) ***Revelation 21:7 Emphasis Mine***

The reason today's believer (as I have mentioned before) must look back at the "cross" is because the "cross" is the means to everything that is available to them. While looking back at the "cross," we must put all our trust, confidence, and faith in "**The Finished Work of Jesus Christ**" who is the source of all the one will ever need in life.

While Jesus was speaking to the disciples, He made it abundantly clear of the only way to salvation and a life of victory.

> "***And He said to them all, If any man come after Me***, (He is speaking of any who are seeking Salvation) ***let him deny himself***, (to deny oneself, is to remove oneself from living within their own strength, knowledge and ability*) **and take up his cross*** (notice, it is the cross of the believing sinner, which is becoming partakers of the benefits of what Jesus Christ accomplished) ***daily*** (everyday in the life of believer) ***and follow Me.*** (That is to live in and walk within the likeness of Jesus Christ)." ***Luke 9:23 Emphasis Mine***

Once the believer begins to do exactly as Jesus instructed, they, through the Holy Spirit, begin to live a life of victory which Jesus Christ accomplished at Calvary. This is the true gospel (see 1 Corinthians 1:17–18, 23; Colossians 2:14). Again, it is through the cross and what Jesus did there and His resurrection that life and it more abundantly is provided.

> "***The thief cometh not, but to steal, and to kill, and to destroy***: (the thief which is Satan and all

his minions are trying to present other avenues (means) to salvation, but there is only one way): ***I am come that they might have life***, (They, are those who seek Jesus Christ as the means for salvation) ***and that they might have it more abundantly." John 10:10 Emphasis Mine***

The "**Abundant Life**" Jesus spoke of is revealed in Romans chapter 6. The apostle Paul referred to it as "**The Newness of Life**" which presents to the believer a "**Brand New Way of Living.**" What a promise to look back too and bring it into the now! I love the way apostle Paul put it;

"That I may know Him, and the power of His resurrection, and the fellowship of His sufferings, being made conformable unto His death." Philippians 3:10

Let's take a closer look into what Paul was revealing. The phrase "*That I may know Him*" is from the Greek word "*ginosko,*" meaning to know experientially, to know, to be acquainted with. This comes with the idea of knowing Jesus Christ and what He did at the Cross, however, it is not a head knowledge but rather knowing Him intimately, and experience His Victory!

The term "*and the power of His resurrection,*" the word "*power*" is from the Greek word "*dunamis,*" which means, power, especially inherent power. This has the basic meaning of being capable, which stresses the factuality of the ability. This refers to the result of the resurrection of Christ which provides the "*newness of life*" i.e. abundant Life (living) and being raised with Christ which is found in Romans 6. This is not speaking of the resurrection to come but of the resurrection of Christ which the believer can be a partaker of now.

The term "*and the fellowship of His sufferings*" is from the following definitions: the word, "*fellowship*" is from the Greek word "*koinonia*" to fellowship with, participate, have communion with. The word "*sufferings*" is from the Greek word "*pathema,*" meaning, to suffer, however, the suffix "*ma*" makes it that which is suffered. With this, the term "*Fellowship of His sufferings*" refers to the believer placing his/her faith and trust in what Jesus Christ accomplished for them. It is also referring to receiving and walking in the "*benefits*" of what Christ has done for us.

The term "*being made conformable unto His death*" is to understand what Christ did and conform to that. It is also coming to the revelation, through what Christ did and is the only way to salvation and sanctification! When the believer begins to walk in this revelation, it allows the Holy Spirit to be the leader in their life (see Romans chapters 6 and 8).

In all the years of ministry, I had placed my faith on what God can do and what He will do. I had thought that I knew what faith was and how to walk in it until several years ago. It was revealed to me, in order to walk in a life of victory, the object of my faith had to be (this was not a suggestion) placed within, "**The Cross and the Finished Work of Jesus Christ.**" It wasn't that my faith was wrong, it was just misplaced. Which brings us back to the scripture used in the heading of this chapter.

"*Looking unto Jesus, the author and finisher of our faith.*" Notice, that Faith began in Jesus Christ (it was always a part of Him) and faith is finished in Him. If it is finished in Him, then there is nothing else that needs to be added to it. Jesus finished it, now we (the believers) must walk in what has been finished. It is not so much your faith that needs to be built up as it is you and I needing built up in our faith.

> "*But ye, beloved, building up yourselves on your most holy faith, praying in the Holy Ghost.*" Jude verse 20

* * * * *

The Challenge

Closely read and study Romans chapters 5, 6, 7, and 8.
Allow the Holy Spirit to bring to you the Revelation of the Finished Work of Jesus Christ
For He (Jesus Christ) said, "It is finished."

Conclusion

There is a mountain of inheritance just waiting on you (the believer) to claim it and obtain it. You may have to face a diversity of obstacles and distractions on your journey. I am totally convinced that every believer can reach that mountain (the things God has promised). There are some who may try to tell you that you are embarking on an impossible task, but don't listen. You have a God-given destiny before you; make the right choices, so you can obtain it. The scriptures proclaim that the steps of a good man are ordered of the Lord. While that is true, you as a believer are still responsible to walk in the path that God has ordered. Finding that path in life may be filled with some twists and turns, and at each of these places a decision must be made on the way which we must travel. That road to travel is the **"Finished Work of Jesus Christ at Calvary."** However, just like Caleb, you may have to endure some hard times and places. You may have to go through a wilderness experience for a season. But, God turns that wilderness into a place of flourishing. He can, and often does, take the desert and makes it a river of living water. Wherever you may find yourself, hang in there and allow God to bring you through with victory.

I want to encourage you to hang onto the vision that God has given you. I can't tell you when your vision becomes a reality, but I can assure you, it comes to pass that is if you continue and not grow weary in well-doing. I have given you what the Holy Spirit placed in me concerning some of the characteristics of Caleb that kept him going. Caleb did reach and obtain his mountain and so can you! You have come too far to let go of your mountain!

KEEP SEEKING AND HOLDING ON TO YOUR MOUNTAIN!

About the Author

Dr. Baldock is the founder/president of Gaining the Victory Ministries. He is currently in his forty-eighth year of ministry.

Dr. Baldock began his ministry in March of 1971. In March of 1973, he began in full time ministry. He and his wife Julie have been married for thirty-four years. Together, they have seven grown children, Rick, Tammy, Tracy, Rhonda, Alicia, Michael, and Ashley. He and Julie also have several grandchildren and great-grandchildren.

Dr. Baldock has pastored nine churches; four of which, he pioneered and built from the ground floor up. Dr. Baldock also has four earned doctorate degrees, and one honorary doctorate.

He is currently traveling around to different churches teaching and preaching the word of God. Dr. Baldock has spoke at many conventions and has worked with several well-known ministries. He taught for several years with the International College of Bible Theology and with Midwest Seminary. He has taught undergraduate and graduate school. He taught at the School of the Prophets in Poplar Bluff, Missouri, for about four years and he taught about two to three years at The Lion of Judah in Malden, Missouri.

Dr. Baldock also traveled to Malawi in East Africa, and for thirteen days, he and two other ministers trained over one hundred and twenty-five church leaders.

Dr. Baldock is a gifted preacher and teacher of the word of God and raised up leaders in the local church. He enjoys helping to restore. He enjoys working with pastors and church leaders to train pastors and leaders who have fallen on hard times and are in need of mentoring.

Dr. Baldock has authored many books and study helps. He believes that the gifts that God has given him should be shared and imparted to (with) others. He believes in everyday, practical teaching that reveals the application of the word of God in the person's everyday living. He is a strong believer to the fact that everything you will ever receive from God is because of the "cross" and "the finished work of Jesus Christ."

He believes that the "cross" is the means of all you will ever need and that "Jesus Christ is the Source" of all that God has supplied for us.

Dr. Baldock is available to speak and teach at your local church or, conferences, along with leadership training and motivational speaking. If you would like for Dr. Baldock to come and speak at your church or conference, and if you would like more information about his books, CDs, DVDs, and a plethora of teaching tools, you can write to:

Gaining the Victory Ministries, Inc.
Dr. R. Michael Baldock
P.O. Box 648
Spencer, Indiana 47460

Or you can e-mail Dr. Baldock at:
gainingvictoryministries@gmail.com

Visit our web site at:
gainingvictoryministries.org

Milton Keynes UK
Ingram Content Group UK Ltd.
UKHW021700290724
1069UKWH00060B/641